Yours truly
John G. Saxe.

POEMS

BY

JOHN G. SAXE.

NINTH EDITION.

BOSTON:
TICKNOR AND FIELDS.
M DCCC LV.

TO HON. GEORGE P. MARSH,

UNITED STATES MINISTER RESIDENT AT CONSTANTINOPLE.

Dear Sir,

I dedicate this little Volume to you, not in your capacity as the honored Representative of your country at a Foreign Court, nor yet in your higher character, as one of the foremost scholars of the age; but rather, as is mere befitting, in token of my esteem for your private virtues, and in grateful acknowledgment of your personal friendship. I hesitate less to avail myself of your kind permission to use your name in this place, since it was greatly owing to your flattering judgment of my first elaborate essay at verse writing, that other pieces were subsequently undertaken, and that these are now here collected. In christening the book, I have chosen, for several reasons, to conform to the customary nomenclature which allows every kind of literature to be 'Poetry,' that is not written in the fashion of prose; yet I have no quarrel with that nicer rule of modern criticism which assigns to all metrical compositions of a mainly facetious or satirical character, a place rather on the border than fairly within the domain of legitimate poesy. If I have excluded several trifles which some of my friends would like to have seen with the rest, it was because I could not afford to make the volume larger at any risk of making it worse. Should the verses which I have ventured to retain, receive, in their present form, the favor which has been accorded to most of the poems separately, I am very sure no one will be more gratified than yourself, — except it be

Your sincere Friend, and humble Servant,

JOHN GODFREY SAXE.

Burlington, Vermont, 1849.

CONTENTS.

PROGRESS: A SATIRE.

POEMS.

PROGRESS:

A SATIRE.

In this, our happy and 'progressive' age,
When all alike ambitious cares engage;
When beardless boys to sudden sages grow,
And 'Miss' her nurse abandons for a beau;
When for their dogmas Non-Resistants fight,
When dunces lecture, and when dandies write
When, martial honors to the children thrown,
Each five-foot minor is a 'Major' grown;
When matrons, seized with oratoric pangs,
Give happy birth to masculine harangues,
And spinsters, trembling for the nation's fate,
Neglect their stockings to preserve the State;

When critic-wits their brazen lustre shed
On golden authors whom they never read,
With parrot praise of 'Roman grandeur' speak,
And in bad English eulogize the Greek;
When facts like these no reprehension bring,
May not, uncensured, an Attorney sing?
In sooth he may; and though 'unborn' to climb
Parnassus' heights, and 'build the lofty rhyme,'
Though FLACCUS fret, and warningly advise
That 'middling verses gods and men despise,'
Yet will he sing, to Yankee licensé true,
In spite of Horace and 'Minerva' too!

My theme is PROGRESS, — never-tiring theme
Of prosing dulness, and poetic dream;
Beloved of Optimists, who still protest
Whatever happens, happens for the best;
Who prate of 'evil' as a thing unknown,
A fancied color, or a seeming tone,
A vague chimera cherished by the dull,
The empty product of an emptier skull.
Expert logicians they! — to show at will,
By ill philosophy, that nought is ill!
Should some sly rogue, the city's constant curse,
Deplete your pocket and relieve your purse,

Or if, approaching with ill-omened tread,
Some bolder burglar break your house and head,
Hold, friend, thy rage! nay, let the rascal flee,
No evil has been done the world, or thee:
Here comes Philosophy will make it plain
Thy seeming loss is universal gain!
'Thy heap of gold was clearly grown too great, —
'Twere best the poor should share thy large estate;
While misers gather, that the knaves should steal,
Is most conducive to the general weal;
Thus thieves the wrongs of avarice efface,
And stand the friends and stewards of the race;
Thus every moral ill but serves, in fact,
Some other equal ill to counteract.'
Sublime Philosophy! — benignant light!
Which sees in every pair of wrongs, a right;
Which finds no evil or in sin or pain,
And proves that decalogues are writ in vain!

Hail, mighty PROGRESS! — loftiest we find
Thy stalking strides in science of the mind.
What boots it now that LOCKE was learned and wise?
What boots it now that men have ears and eyes?
'Pure Reason' in their stead now hears and sees,
And walks apart in stately scorn of these;

Laughs at 'experience,' spurns 'induction' hence,
Scouting 'the senses,' and transcending sense.
No more shall flippant ignorance inquire,
'If German breasts may feel poetic fire,'
Nor German dulness write ten folios full
To show, for once, that Dutchmen are not dull.[1]
For here Philosophy, acute, refined,
Sings all the marvels of the human mind
In strains so passing 'dainty sweet' to hear,
That e'en the nursery turns a ravished ear!
Here Wit and Fancy in scholastic bowers,
Twine beauteous wreaths of metaphysic flowers;
Here Speculation pours her dazzling light,
Here grand Invention wings a daring flight,
And soars ambitious to the lofty moon,
Whence, haply, freighted with some precious boon
Some old 'Philosophy' in fog incased,
Or new 'Religion' for the changing taste,
She straight descends to Learning's blest abodes,
Just simultaneous with the Paris modes!
Here PLATO's dogmas eloquently speak,
Not as of yore, in grand and graceful Greek,
But, (quite beyond the dreaming sage's hope
Of future glory in his fancy's scope,)
Translated *down*, as by some wizard touch,
Find 'immortality' in good high Dutch!

Happy the youth, in this our golden age,
Condemned no more to con the prosy page
Of LOCKE and BACON, antiquated fools
Now justly banished from our moral schools.
By easier modes philosophy is taught,
Than through the medium of laborious thought.
Imagination kindly serves instead,
And saves the pupil many an aching head.
Room for the sages! — hither comes a throng
Of blooming Platos trippingly along.
In dress how fitted to beguile the fair!
What intellectual, stately heads — of hair!
Hark to the Oracle! — to Wisdom's tone
Breathed in a fragrant zephyr of Cologne.
That boy in gloves, the leader of the van,
Talks of the 'outer' and the 'inner man,'
And knits his girlish brow in stout resolve
Some mountain-sized 'idea' to 'evolve.'
Delusive toil! — thus in their infant days,
When children mimic manly deeds in plays,
Long will they sit, and eager, 'bob for whale,'
Within the ocean of a water pail!
The next, whose looks unluckily reveal
The ears portentous that his locks conceal,
Prates of the 'orbs' with such a knowing frown,
You deem he puffs some lithographic town

In Western wilds, where yet unbroken ranks
Of thrifty beavers build unchartered 'banks,'
And prowling panthers occupy the lots
Adorned with churches on the paper plots!
But ah! what suff'ring harp is this we hear?
What jarring sounds invade the wounded ear?
Who o'er the lyre a hand spasmodic flings,
And grinds harsh discord from the tortured strings?
The Sacred Muses at the sound dismayed,
Retreat disordered to their native shade,
And PHŒBUS hastens to his high abode,
And ORPHEUS frowns to hear an 'Orphic ode!'

Talk not, ye jockeys, of the wondrous speed
That marks your northern or your southern steed:
See Progress fly o'er Education's course!
Not far-famed Derby owns a fleeter horse!
On rare Improvement's 'short and easy' road,
How swift her flight to Learning's blest abode!
In other times, — 'twas many years ago, —
The scholar's course was toilsome, rough, and slow,
The fair Humanities were sought in tears,
And came, the trophy of laborious years.
Now Learning's shrine each idle youth may seek,
And, spending there a shilling and a week,

(At lightest cost of study, cash, and lungs,)
Come back, like *Rumor*, with a hundred tongues!

What boots such progress, when the golden load
From heedless haste is lost upon the road?
When each great science, to the student's pace,
Stands like the wicket, in a hurdle race,
Which to o'erleap, is all the courser's mind,
And all his glory, that 'tis left behind!

Nor less, O Progress, are thy newest rules
Enforced and honored in the 'Ladies' Schools;'
Where Education, in its nobler sense,
Gives place to Learning's shallowest pretence;
Where hapless maids, in spite of wish or taste,
On vain 'accomplishments' their moments waste;
By cruel parents here condemned to wrench
Their tender throats in mispronouncing French;
Here doomed to force, by unrelenting knocks,
Reluctant music from a tortured box;
Here taught, in inky shades and rigid lines,
To perpetrate equivocal 'designs;'
'Drawings' that prove their title plainly true,
By showing nature 'drawn,' and 'quartered' too!

In ancient times, I've heard my grandam tell,
Young maids were taught to read, and write, and spell;
(Neglected arts! once learned by rigid rules,
As prime essentials in the 'common schools.')
Well taught beside in many a useful art
To mend the manners and improve the heart;
Nor yet unskilled to turn the busy wheel,
To ply the shuttle, and to twirl the reel,
Could thrifty tasks with cheerful grace pursue,
Themselves 'accomplished,' and their duties too.
Of tongues, each maiden had but one, 'tis said,
(Enough, 'twas thought, to serve a lady's head,)
But that was ENGLISH, — great and glorious tongue
That CHATHAM spoke, and MILTON, SHAKSPEARE, sung!
Let thoughts too idle to be fitly dressed
In sturdy Saxon, be in French expressed;
Let lovers breathe Italian, — like, in sooth,
Its singers, soft, emasculate, and smooth;
But for a tongue, whose ample powers embrace
Beauty and force, sublimity and grace,
Ornate or plain, harmonious, yet strong,
And formed alike for eloquence and song,
Give me the ENGLISH, — aptest tongue to paint
A sage or dunce, a villain or a saint,

To spur the slothful, counsel the distressed,
To lash the oppressor, and to soothe the oppressed,
To lend fantastic Humor freest scope
To marshal all his laughter-moving troop,
Give Pathos power, and Fancy lightest wings,
And Wit his merriest whims and keenest stings!

The march of Progress let the Muse explore
In pseudo-science, and empiric lore.
O, sacred Science! how art thou profaned,
When shallow quacks, and vagrants, unrestrained,
Flaunt in thy robes, and vagabonds are known
To brawl thy name, who never wrote their own;
When crazy theorists their addled schemes,
(Unseemly product of dyspeptic dreams,)
Impute to thee! — as courtesans of yore
Their spurious bantlings left at Mars's door;
When each projector of a patent pill,
Or happy founder of a coffee-mill,
Invokes thine aid to celebrate his wares,
And crown with gold his philanthropic cares;
Thus Islam's hawkers piously proclaim
Their figs and pippins in the Prophet's name!

Some sage Physician, studious to advance
The art of healing, and its praise enhance,

By observation 'scientific,' finds,
(What else were hidden from inferior minds,)
That WATER's useful in a thousand ways,
To cherish health, and lengthen out our days;
A mighty solvent in its simple scope,
And quite 'specific' with Castilian soap!
The doctor's labors let the thoughtless scorn,
See! a new 'science' to the world is born;
'Disease is dirt! all pain the patient feels
Is but the soiling of the vital wheels;
To wash away all particles impure,
And cleanse the system, plainly is to cure!'
Thus shouts the doctor, eloquent, and proud
To teach his 'science' to the gaping crowd;
Like 'Father Mathew,' eager to allure
Afflicted mortals to his 'water cure!'

'Tis thus that modern 'sciences' are made,
By bold assumption, puffing, and parade.
Take three stale 'truths;' a dozen 'facts,' assumed;
Two known 'effects,' and fifty more presumed;
'Affinities' a score, to sense unknown,
And, just as '*lucus, non lucendo*' shown,
Add but a name of pompous Anglo-Greek,
And only not impossible to speak,

The work is done; a 'science' stands confest,
And countless welcomes greet the queenly guest

In closest girdle, O reluctant Muse,
In scantiest skirts, and lightest-stepping shoes,[2]
Prepare to follow FASHION's gay advance,
And thread the mazes of her motley dance;
And marking well each momentary hue,
And transient form, that meets the wondering view,
In kindred colors, gentle Muse, essay
Her Protean phases fitly to portray.
To-day, she slowly drags a cumbrous trail,
And 'Tom' rejoices in its length of tail;
To-morrow, changing her capricious sport,
She trims her flounces just as much too short;
To-day, right jauntily, a hat she wears
That scarce affords a shelter to her ears;
To-morrow, haply, searching long in vain,
You spy her features down a Leghorn lane;
To-day, she glides along with queenly grace,
To-morrow, ambles in a mincing pace;
To-day, erect, she loves a martial air,
And envious train-bands emulate the fair;
To-morrow, changing as her whim may serve,
'She stoops to conquer' in a 'Grecian curve.'[3]

To-day, with careful negligence arrayed,
In scanty folds of woven zephyrs made,
She moves like Dian in her woody bowers,
Or Flora floating o'er a bed of flowers;
To-morrow, laden with a motley freight
Of startling bulk and formidable weight,
She waddles forth, ambitious to amaze
The vulgar crowd, who giggle as they gaze!

Despotic Fashion! potent is her sway,
Whom half the world full loyally obey,
Kings bow submissive to her stern decrees,
And proud Republics bend their necks and knees;
Where'er we turn the attentive eye, is seen
The worshipped presence of the modish queen!
In Dress, Philosophy, Religion, Art,
Whate'er employs the head, or hand, or heart.

In some fine lady quite o'ercome with woes,
From an unyielding pimple on her nose, —
Some unaccustomed 'buzzing in her ears,'
Or other marvel to alarm her fears?
Fashion, with skill and judgment ever nice,
At once advises 'medical advice;'
Then names her doctor, who, arrived in haste,
Proceeds accordant with the laws of taste.

If real ills afflict the modish dame,
Her blind idolatry is still the same;
Less grievous far, she deems it, to endure
Genteel mal-practice, than a vulgar cure.
If, spits of gilded pills and golden fees,
Her dear dyspepsia grows a dire disease,
And Doctor DAPPER proves a shallow rogue,
The world must own that both were much in vogue!

What impious mockery, when, with soulless art,
Fashion, intrusive, seeks to rule the heart;
Directs how grief may tastefully be borne;
Instructs Bereavement just how long to mourn;
Shows Sorrow how by nice degrees to fade,
And marks its measure in a ribbon's shade!
More impious still, when, through her wanton laws,
She desecrates Religion's sacred cause;
Shows how 'the narrow road' is easiest trod,
And how, genteelest, worms may worship God;
How sacred rites may bear a worldly grace,
And self-abasement wear a haughty face;
How sinners, long in Folly's mazes whirled,
With pomp and splendor may 'renounce the world;'
How, 'with all saints hereafter to appear,'
Yet quite escape the vulgar portion here!

Imperial Fashion! her impartial care,
Things most momentous, and most trivial, share.
Now crushing conscience (her invet'rate foe),
And now a waist, and now, perchance, a toe;
At once for pistols and 'the Polka' votes,
And shapes alike our characters and coats;
The gravest question which the world divides,
And lightest riddle, in a breath decides:
'If wrong may not, by circumstance, be right,' —
'If black cravats be more genteel than white,' —
'If, by her "bishop," or her "grace," alone,
A genuine lady, or a church, is known;' —
Problems like these, she solves with graceful air,
At once a casuist and a connoisseur!

Does some sleek knave, whom magic money-bags
Have raised above his fellow-knaves in rags,
Some willing minion of unblushing Vice,
Who boasts that 'Virtue ever has her price,' —
Does he, unpitying, blast thy sister's fame,
Or doom thy daughter to undying shame,
To bow her head beneath the eye of scorn,
And droop and wither in her maiden morn?
Fashion 'regrets,' declares ''twas very wrong,'
And, quite dejected, hums an opera song!

Impartial friend! your cause to her appealed,
Yourself and foe she summons to the field,
Where Honor carefully the case observes,
And nicely weighs it in a scale of nerves!
Despotic rite! whose fierce vindictive reign
Boasts, unrebuked, its countless victims slain,
While Christian rulers, recreant, support
The pagan honors of thy bloody court,
And 'Freedom's champions' spurn their hallowed trust,
Kneel at thy nod, and basely lick the dust!

Degraded Congress! once the honored scene
Of patriot deeds; where men of solemn mien,
In virtue strong, in understanding clear,
Earnest, though courteous, and though smooth, sincere,
To gravest counsels lent the teeming hours,
And gave their country all their mighty powers.
But times are changed; a rude, degenerate race
Usurp the seats, and shame the sacred place.
Here plotting demagogues, with zeal defend
The 'people's rights,' — to gain some private end;
Here southern youths, on Folly's surges tost,
Their fathers' wisdom eloquently boast;
(So dowerless spinsters proudly number o'er
The costly jewels that their grandams wore.)

Here, would-be TULLYS pompously parade
Their tumid tropes for simple 'Buncombe' made,[4]
Full on the chair the chilling torrent shower,
And work their word-pumps through the allotted hour.
Deluded 'Buncombe!' while, with honest praise,
She notes each grand and patriotic phrase,
And, much rejoicing in her hopeful son,
Deems all her own the laurels he has won,
She little dreams how brother members fled,
And left the house as vacant as his head!
Here rural CHATHAMS, eager to attest
The 'growing greatness of the mighty West,'
To make the plainest proposition clear,
Crack PRISCIAN'S head, and Mr. SPEAKER'S ear;
Then closing up in one terrific shout,
Pour all their 'wild-cats' furiously out!
Here lawless boors with ruffian bullies vie,
Who last shall give the rude, insulting, 'lie,'
While 'Order! order!' loud the chairman calls,
And echoing 'Order,' every member bawls;
Till rising high in rancorous debate,
And higher still in fierce envenomed hate,[5]
Retorted blows the scene of riot crown,
And big LYCURGUS knocks the lesser down!

Ye honest dames in frequent proverbs named,
For finest fish and foulest English famed,
Whose matchless tongues, 'tis said, were never heard
To speak a flattering or a feeble word, —
Here all your choice invective ye might urge
Our lawless *Solons* fittingly to scourge;
Here, in congenial company, might rail
Till quite worn out your creaking voices fail —
Unless, indeed, for once compelled to yield
In wordy strife, ye vanquished quit the field!

Hail, Social Progress! each new moon is rife
With some new theory of social life,
Some matchless scheme ingeniously designed
From half their miseries to free mankind;
On human wrongs triumphant war to wage,
And bring anew the glorious golden age.
'Association' is the magic word
From many a social 'priest and prophet' heard;
'Attractive Labor' is the angel given,
To render earth a sublunary Heaven!
'Attractive Labor!' ring the changes round,
And labor grows attractive in the sound;
And many a youthful mind, where haply lurk
Unwelcomed fancies at the name of 'work,'

Sees pleasant pastime in its longing view
Of 'toil made easy' and 'attractive' too,
And, fancy-rapt, with joyful ardor, turns
Delightful grindstones, and seductive churns!
'Men are not bad,' these social sages preach,
'Men are not what their actions seem to teach;
No moral ill is natural or fixed,—
Men only err by being badly mixed!'
To them the world a huge plum-pudding seems,
Made up of richest viands, fruits and creams,
Which of all choice ingredients partook,
And then was ruined by a blundering cook!

Inventive France! what wonder-working schemes
Astound the world whene'er a Frenchman dreams.
What fine-spun theories,—ingenious, new,
Sublime, stupendous, every thing but true!
One little favor, O 'Imperial France,'
Still teach the world to cook, to dress, to dance;
Let, if thou wilt, thy boots and barbers roam,
But keep thy morals and thy creeds at home!

O, might the Muse prolong her flowing rhyme,
(Too closely cramped by unrelenting Time,
Whose dreadful scythe swings heedlessly along,
And, missing speeches, clips the thread of song,)

How would she strive, in fitting verse, to sing
The wondrous Progress of the Printing King!
Bibles and Novels, Treatises and Songs,
Lectures on 'Rights,' and Strictures upon Wrongs;
Verse in all metres, Travels in all climes,
Rhymes without reason, Sonnets without rhymes;
'Translations from the French,' so vilely done,
The wheat escaping, leaves the chaff alone;
Memoirs, where dunces sturdily essay
To cheat Oblivion of her certain prey;
Critiques, where pedants vauntingly expose
Unlicensed verses, in unlawful prose;
Lampoons, whose authors strive in vain to throw
Their headless arrows from a nerveless bow;
Poems by youths, who, crossing Nature's will,
Harangue the landscape they were born to till;
Huge tomes of Law, that lead by rugged routes
Through ancient dogmas down to modern doubts;
Where Judges, oft, with well-affected ease,
Give learned reasons for absurd decrees,
Or, more ingenious still, contrive to found
Some just decision on fallacious ground,
Or blink the point, and, haply, in its place,
Moot and decide some hypothetic case;
Smart Epigrams, all sadly out of joint,
And pointless, — save the 'exclamation point,'

Which stands in state, with vacant wonder fraught,
The pompous tombstone of some pauper thought;
Ingenious systems based on doubtful facts,
'Tracts for the Times,' and most untimely tracts;
Polemic Pamphlets, Literary Toys,
And Easy Lessons for uneasy boys;
Hebdomadal Gazettes, and Daily News,
Gay Magazines, and Quarterly Reviews;
Small portion these, of all the vast array
Of darkened leaves that cloud each passing day,
And pour their tide unceasingly along,
A gathering, swelling, overwhelming throng!

Cease, O my Muse, nor, indiscreet, prolong
To epic length thy unambitious song.
Good friends, be gentle to a maiden muse,
Her errors pardon, and her faults excuse.
Not uninvited to her task she came,[6]
To sue for favor, not to seek for fame.
Be this, at least, her just though humble praise,
No stale excuses heralded her lays,
No singers' trick — conveniently to bring
A sudden cough, when importuned to sing:[7]
No deprecating phrases, learned by rote, —
'She'd quite forgot,' or 'never knew a note,' —

But to her task, with ready zeal addressed
Her earnest care, and aimed to do her best;
Strove to be just in each satiric word,
To doubtful wit, undoubted truth preferred,
To please and profit equally has aimed,
Nor been ill-natured, even when she blamed.

NOTES.

NOTE 1. Page 14.

'To show for once, that Dutchmen are not dull.'

Pere Bouhours seriously asked 'if a German could be a "*bel esprit*." This concise question was answered by Kramer, in a ponderous work entitled '*Vindiciæ nominis Germanicæ*.'

NOTE 2. Page 21.

'In closest girdle, O reluctant Muse,
In scantiest skirts and lightest-stepping shoes.'

Imitated from the opening couplet of Holmes's 'Terpsichore,'

'In narrowest girdle, O reluctant Muse,
In closest frock and Cinderella shoes.'

NOTE 3. Page 21.

'She stoops to conquer in a Grecian curve.'

Terence, who wrote comedies a little more than two thousand years ago, thus alludes to this and a kindred custom *then* prevalent among the Roman girls:—

——————— 'virgines, quas matres student
Demissis humeris esse, vincto corpore, ut graciles fiant.'

The sense of the passage may be given in English, with sufficient accuracy, thus:—

Maidens, whom fond, maternal care has graced
With stooping shoulders, and a cinctured waist.

Note 4. Page 26.

'*Their tumid tropes for simple Buncombe made.*'

Many readers, who have heard about 'making speeches for Buncombe,' may not be aware that the phrase originated as follows: — A member of Congress from the county of Buncombe, North Carolina, while pronouncing a magniloquent set-speech, was interrupted by a remark from the chair, that 'the seats were quite vacant.' 'Never mind, never mind,' replied the orator, 'I'm talking for Buncombe!'

Note 5. Page 28.

'*Till rising high in rancorous debate,*
And higher still in fierce, envenomed hate,'
Etc.

——————— Sed jurgia prima sonare
Incipiunt animis ardentibus; hæc tuba rixæ;
Dein clamore pari concurritur, et vice teli
Sævit nuda manus. — Juv. Sat. xv.

Note 6. Page 30.

'*Not uninvited to her task she came.*'

This Poem was written at the instance of the Associated Alumni of Middlebury College, and spoken before that Society, July 22, 1846.

Note 7. Page 30.

'*No singers' trick, — conveniently to bring*
A sudden cough when importuned to sing.'

The capriciousness of musical folk, here alluded to, is by no means peculiar to our times. A little before the Christian era, Horace had occasion to scold the Roman singers for the same fault: —

'*Omnibus hoc vitium est cantoribus, inter amicos,*
Ut nunquam inducant animum cantare rogati;
Injussi nunquam desistant.' — Sat. iii.

THE PROUD MISS MAC BRIDE.

THE PROUD MISS MAC BRIDE

A LEGEND OF GOTHAM.

I.

O, TERRIBLY proud was Miss Mac Bride,
The very personification of Pride,
As she minced along in Fashion's tide,
Adown Broadway, — on the proper side, —
When the golden sun was setting;
There was pride in the head she carried so high,
Pride in her lip, and pride in her eye,
And a world of pride in the very sigh
That her stately bosom was fretting;

II.

A sigh that a pair of elegant feet,
Sandaled in satin, should kiss the street, —
The very same that the vulgar greet
In common leather not over 'neat,' —
For such is the common booting;

(And Christian tears may well be shed,
That even among our gentlemen bred,
The glorious day of Morocco is dead,
And Day and Martin are raining instead,
    On a much inferior footing!)

III.

O, terribly proud was Miss Mac Bride,
Proud of her beauty, and proud of her pride,
And proud of fifty matters beside
    That wouldn't have borne dissection;
Proud of her wit, and proud of her walk,
Proud of her teeth, and proud of her talk,
Proud of 'knowing cheese from chalk,'
    On a very slight inspection!

IV.

Proud abroad, and proud at home,
Proud wherever she chanced to come,
When she was glad, and when she was glum.
    Proud as the head of a Saracen
Over the door of a tippling shop!—
Proud as a duchess, proud as a fop,
'Proud as a boy with a bran-new top,'
    Proud beyond comparison!

V.

It seems a singular thing to say,
But her very senses led her astray
    Respecting all humility;
In sooth, her dull auricular drum
Could find in *Humble* only a 'hum,'
And heard no sound of 'gentle' come,
    In talking about gentility.

VI.

What *Lowly* meant she didn't know,
For she always avoided 'every thing low,'
    With care the most punctilious,
And queerer still, the audible sound
Of 'super-silly' she never had found
    In the adjective supercilious!

VII.

The meaning of *Meek* she never knew,
But imagined the phrase had something to do
With 'Moses,'—a peddling German Jew,
Who, like all hawkers the country through,
    Was a person of no position;
And it seemed to her exceedingly plain,
If the word was really known to pertain
To a vulgar German, it wasn't germane
    To a lady of high condition!

VIII.

Even her graces, — not her grace,
For that was in the 'vocative case,' —
Chilled with the touch of her icy face,
    Sat very stiffly upon her;
She never confessed a favor aloud,
Like one of the simple, common crowd,
But coldly smiled, and faintly bowed,
As who should say: 'You do me proud,
    And do yourself an honor!'

IX.

And yet the pride of Miss Mac Bride,
Although it had fifty hobbies to ride,
    Had really no foundation;
But like the fabrics that gossips devise, —
Those single stories that often arise
And grow till they reach a four-story size,
    Was merely a fancy creation!

X.

'Tis a curious fact as ever was known
In human nature, but often shown
    Alike in castle and cottage,
That pride, like pigs of a certain breed,
Will manage to live and thrive on 'feed'
    As poor as a pauper's pottage!

XI.

That her wit should never have made her vain,
Was, like her face, sufficiently plain ;
And as to her musical powers,
Although she sang until she was hoarse,
And issued notes with a Banker's force,
They were just such notes as we never indorse
For any acquaintance of ours !

XII.

Her birth, indeed, was uncommonly high,
For Miss Mac Bride first opened her eye
Through a sky-light dim, on the light of the sky;
But pride is a curious passion,
And in talking about her wealth and worth,
She always forgot to mention her birth,
To people of rank and fashion !

XIII.

Of all the notable things on earth,
The queerest one is pride of birth,
Among our 'fierce Democracie !'
A bridge across a hundred years,
Without a prop to save it from sneers, —
Not even a couple of rotten Peers, —
A thing for laughter, fleers and jeers,
Is American aristocracy !

XIV.

English and Irish, French and Spanish,
German, Italian, Dutch and Danish,
Crossing their veins until they vanish
In one conglomeration!
So subtle a tangle of Blood, indeed,
No heraldry-Harvey will ever succeed
In finding the circulation!

XV.

Depend upon it, my snobbish friend,
Your family thread you can't ascend,
Without good reason to apprehend
You may find it waxed at the farther end
By some plebeian vocation!
Or, worse than that, your boasted Line
May end in a loop of stronger twine,
That plagued some worthy relation!

XVI.

But Miss Mac Bride hath something beside
Her lofty birth to nourish her pride, —
For rich was the old paternal Mac Bride,
According to public rumor;
And he lived 'Up Town,' in a splendid Square,
And kept his daughter on dainty fare,

And gave her gems that were rich and rare,
And the finest rings and things to wear,
    And feathers enough to plume her!

XVII.

An honest mechanic was John Mac Bride,
As ever an honest calling plied,
    Or graced an honest ditty;
For John had worked in his early day,
In 'Pots and Pearls,' the legends say,
And kept a shop with a rich array
Of things in the soap and candle way,
    In the lower part of the city.

XVIII.

No *rara avis* was honest John,
(That's the Latin for 'sable swan,')
    Though in one of his fancy flashes,
A wicked wag, who meant to deride,
Called honest John 'Old *Phœnix* Mac Bride,'
    'Because he rose from his ashes!'

XIX.

Little by little he grew to be rich,
By saving of candle-ends and 'sich,'
Till he reached, at last, an opulent niche,—
    No very uncommon affair;

For history quite confirms the law
Expressed in the ancient Scottish saw,
A MICKLE may come to be May'r ! [1]

XX.

Alack ! for many ambitious beaux !
She hung their hopes upon her nose, —
(The figure is quite Horatian !) [2]
Until from habit the member grew
As queer a thing as ever you knew
Turn up to observation !

XXI.

A thriving tailor begged her hand,
But she gave 'the fellow' to understand,
By a violent manual action,
She perfectly scorned the best of his clan,
And reckoned the ninth of any man
An exceedingly Vulgar Fraction !

XXII.

Another, whose sign was a golden boot,
Was mortified with a bootless suit,
In a way that was quite appalling ;

---

[1] Mickle, wi' thrift may chance to be mair.— *Scotch Proverb.* Andrew Mickle, former Mayor of New York.

[2] " Omnia suspendens naso."

For though a regular *sutor* by trade,
He wasn't a suitor to suit the maid,
Who cut him off with a saw, — and bade
'The cobbler keep to his calling.'

XXIII.

(The Muse must let a secret out, —
There isn't the faintest shadow of doubt,
That folks who oftenest sneer and flout
At 'the dirty, low mechanicals,'
Are they whose sires, by pounding their knees,
Or coiling their legs, or trades like these,
Contrived to win their children ease
From poverty's galling manacles.)

XXIV.

A rich tobacconist comes and sues,
And, thinking the lady would scarce refuse
A man of his wealth and liberal views,
Began, at once, with 'If you choose, —
And could you really love him —'
But the lady spoiled his speech in a huff,
With an answer rough and ready enough,
To let him know she was up to snuff,
And altogether above him!

XXV.

A young attorney of winning grace,
Was scarce allowed to 'open his face,'
Ere Miss Mac Bride had closed his case
With true judicial celerity;
For the lawyer was poor, and 'seedy' to boot,
And to say the lady discarded his *suit*,
Is merely a double verity.

XXVI.

The last of those who came to court
Was a lively beau of the dapper sort,
'Without any visible means of support,'
A crime by no means flagrant
In one who wears an elegant coat,
But the very point on which they vote
A ragged fellow 'a vagrant.'

XXVII.

A courtly fellow was Dapper Jim,
Sleek and supple, and tall and trim,
And smooth of tongue as neat of limb,
And maugre his meagre pocket,
You'd say, from the glittering tales he told,
That Jim had slept in a cradle of gold,
With Fortunatus to rock it!

XXVIII.

Now Dapper Jim his courtship plied,
(I wish the fact could be denied,)
With an eye to the purse of the old Mac Bride,
And really 'nothing shorter!'
For he said to himself, in his greedy lust,
'Whenever he dies, — as die he must, —
And yields to Heaven his vital trust,
He's very sure to "come down with his dust,"
In behalf of his only daughter.'

XXIX.

And the very magnificent Miss Mac Bride,
Half in love and half in pride,
Quite graciously relented;
And tossing her head, and turning her back,
No token of proper pride to lack, —
To be a Bride without the 'Mac,'
With much disdain, consented!

XXX.

Alas! that people who've got their box
Of cash beneath the best of locks,
Secure from all financial shocks,
Should stock their fancy with fancy stocks,
And madly rush upon Wall-street rocks,
Without the least apology!

Alas! that people whose money affairs
Are sound beyond all need of repairs,
Should ever tempt the bulls and bears
    Of Mammon's fierce Zoölogy!

XXXI.

Old John Mac Bride, one fatal day,
Became the unresisting prey
    Of Fortune's undertakers;
And staking his all on a single die,
His foundered bark went high and dry
    Among the brokers and breakers!

XXXII.

At his trade again in the very shop
Where, years before, he let it drop,
    He follows his ancient calling, —
Cheerily, too, in poverty's spite,
And sleeping quite as sound at night,
As when at Fortune's giddy height,
He used to wake with a dizzy fright
    From a dismal dream of falling.

XXXIII.

But alas! for the haughty Miss Mac Bride,
'Twas such a shock to her precious pride!
She couldn't recover, although she tried
    Her jaded spirits to rally;

'Twas a dreadful change in human affairs,
From a Place 'Up Town,' to a nook 'Up Stairs,'
From an Avenue down to an Alley!

XXXIV.

'Twas little condolence she had, God wot,
From her 'troops of friends,' who hadn't forgot
The airs she used to borrow;
They had civil phrases enough, but yet
'Twas plain to see that their 'deepest regret'
Was a different thing from Sorrow!

XXXV.

They owned it couldn't have well been worse,
To go from a full to an empty purse,
To expect a reversion and get a 'reverse,'
Was truly a dismal feature;
But it wasn't strange, — they whispered, — at all;
That the Summer of pride should have its Fall.
Was quite according to Nature!

XXXVI.

And one of those chaps who make a pun,
As if it were quite legitimate fun
To be blazing away at every one,
With a regular double-loaded gun, —
Remarked that moral transgression

Always brings retributive stings
To candle-makers, as well as kings:
And making light of cereous things,
Was a very wick-ed profession!

XXXVII.

And vulgar people, the saucy churls,
Inquired about 'the price of Pearls,'
And mocked at her situation;
'She wasn't ruined,—they ventured to hope,—
Because she was poor, she needn't mope,—
Few people were better off for soap,
And that was a consolation!'

XXXVIII.

And to make her cup of woe run over,
Her elegant, ardent, plighted lover,
Was the very first to forsake her;
'He quite regretted the step, 'twas true,—
The lady had pride enough "for two,"
But that alone would never do
To quiet the butcher and baker!'

XXXIX.

And now the unhappy Miss Mac Bride,
The merest ghost of her early pride,
Bewails her lonely position;

Cramped in the very narrowest niche,
Above the poor, and below the rich,
Was ever a worse condition?

MORAL.

Because you flourish in worldly affairs,
Don't be haughty, and put on airs,
With insolent pride of station!
Don't be proud, and turn up your nose
At poorer people in plainer clo'es,
But learn, for the sake of your soul's repose,
That wealth's a bubble, that comes — and goes!
And that all Proud Flesh, wherever it grows,
Is subject to irritation!

THE BRIEFLESS BARRISTER.

A BALLAD.

An Attorney was taking a turn,
  In shabby habiliments drest;
His coat it was shockingly worn,
  And the rust had invested his vest.

His breeches had suffered a breach,
  His linen and worsted were worse;
He had scarce a whole crown in his hat,
  And not half-a-crown in his purse.

And thus as he wandered along,
  A cheerless and comfortless elf,
He sought for relief in a song,
  Or complainingly talked to himself:

'Unfortunate man that I am!
  I've never a client but grief;
The case is, I've no case at all,
  And in brief, I've ne'er had a brief!

'I've waited and waited in vain,
  Expecting an "opening" to find,
Where an honest young lawyer might gain
  Some reward for the toil of his mind.

''Tis not that I'm wanting in law,
  Or lack an intelligent face,
That others have cases to plead,
  While I have to plead for a case.

'O, how can a modest young man
  E'er hope for the smallest progression, —
The profession's already so full
  Of lawyers so full of profession!'

While thus he was strolling around,
  His eye accidentally fell
On a very deep hole in the ground,
  And he sighed to himself, 'It is well!'

To curb his emotions, he sat
  On the curb-stone the space of a minute,
Then cried, 'Here's an opening at last!'
  And in less than a jiffy was in it!

Next morning twelve citizens came,
  ('Twas the coroner bade them attend,)
To the end that it might be determined
  How the man had determined his end!

'The man was a lawyer, I hear,'
  Quoth the foreman who sat on the corse;
'A lawyer? Alas!' said another,
  'Undoubtedly died of remorse!'

A third said, 'He knew the deceased,
  An attorney well versed in the laws,
And as to the cause of his death,
  'Twas no doubt from the want of a cause.'

The jury decided at length,
  After solemnly weighing the matter,
'That the lawyer was drown*d*ed, because
  He could not keep his head above water!'

RHYME OF THE RAIL.

SINGING through the forests,
  Rattling over ridges,
Shooting under arches,
  Rumbling over bridges,
Whizzing through the mountains,
  Buzzing o'er the vale, —
Bless me ! this is pleasant,
  Riding on the Rail !

Men of different 'stations'
  In the eye of Fame,
Here are very quickly
  Coming to the same.
High and lowly people,
  Birds of every feather,
On a common level
  Travelling together !

Gentleman in shorts,
  Looming very tall;
Gentleman at large,
  Talking very small;
Gentleman in tights,
  With a loose-ish mien;
Gentleman in gray,
  Looking rather green.

Gentleman quite old,
  Asking for the news;
Gentleman in black,
  In a fit of blues;
Gentleman in claret,
  Sober as a vicar;
Gentleman in Tweed,
  Dreadfully in liquor!

Stranger on the right,
  Looking very sunny,
Obviously reading
  Something rather funny.
Now the smiles are thicker,
  Wonder what they mean?
Faith, he 's got the KNICKER-
  BOCKER Magazine!

Stranger on the left,
  Closing up his peepers,
Now he snores amain,
  Like the Seven Sleepers;
At his feet a volume
  Gives the explanation,
How the man grew stupid
  From 'Association!'

Ancient maiden lady
  Anxiously remarks,
That there must be peril
  'Mong so many sparks;
Roguish looking fellow,
  Turning to the stranger,
Says it's his opinion
  She is out of danger!

Woman with her baby,
  Sitting vis-a-vis;
Baby keeps a squalling,
  Woman looks at me;
Asks about the distance,
  Says it's tiresome talking,
Noises of the cars
  Are so very shocking!

5

Market woman careful
  Of the precious casket,
Knowing eggs are eggs,
  Tightly holds her basket;
Feeling that a smash,
  If it came, would surely
Sends her eggs to pot
  Rather prematurely!

Singing through the forests,
  Rattling over ridges,
Shooting under arches,
  Rumbling over bridges,
Whizzing through the mountains,
  Buzzing o'er the vale;
Bless me! this is pleasant,
  Riding on the Rail!

THE RAPE OF THE LOCK.

THE RAPE OF THE LOCK;

OR,

CAPTAIN JONES'S MISADVENTURE.

I.

To follow the line of Captain JONES
Back to the old ancestral bones,
Were surely an idle endeavor ·
For all that is known of the family feats,
Is that his sire, as a paver of streets,
Had paved his way in a manner that meets
The appellation of clever.

II.

'Twere pleasant enough more fully to trace
The various steps in the Captain's race,
If the records of heraldy had 'em;
But History leaps at a single span
From the primitive pair to the pavior-man,
From ADAM down to MAC ADAM.

III.

'Twas rumored indeed, but nobody knows
What credit to give to such rumors as those,
His grand-papa was a cooper ;
But getting fatigued with this round-about mode
Of staving through life, he took to the Road,
As a kind of irregular trooper.

IV.

But soon, although a fellow of pluck,
By a singular turn in the wheel of luck,
He met with a mortal miscarriage,
By means of a cord that was dangling loose,
And fell over his head in a dangerous noose,
That wasn't at all like Marriage.

V.

A tale invented by foes, no doubt,
Which idle people had helped about,
Till it went alone, it got so stout ;
For as to the truth of the story,
I scarcely ought to have named it here,
It seems to me so exceedingly clear,
The fable is Newgate-ory.

VI.

And that's the pith of the pedigree
Of Captain Jones, whose family tree
Was a little shrub, 'tis plain to see;
But what the topers mention
Respecting wine, is true of blood:
It 'needs no bush if it's only good,'
Much less a tree of the oldest wood,
To warrant the world's attention.

VII.

Now Captain Jones was a five-feet ten,
(The height of Chesterfield's gentlemen,)
With a manly breadth of shoulder;
And Captain Jones was straight and trim,
With nothing about him anywise slim,
And had for a leg as perfect a limb
As ever astonished beholder!

VIII.

With a calf of such a notable size,
'Twould surely have taken the highest prize
At any fair Fair in creation;
'Twas just the leg for a prince to sport
Who wished to stand at a Royal Court,
At the head of Foreign Leg-ation!

IX.

And Captain JONES had an elegant foot,
'Twas just the thing for his patent boot,
And could so prettily shove it,
'Twas a genuine pleasure to see it repeat
In the public walks the Milonian feat
Of bearing the calf above it!

X.

But the Captain's prominent personal charm
Was neither his foot, nor leg, nor arm,
Nor his very *distingue* air;
Nor was it, although you're thinking upon't,
The front of his head, but his head and front
Of beautiful coal-black hair!

XI.

So very bright was the gloss they had,
'Twould have made a rival raving mad
To look at his raven curls;
Wherever he went, the Captain's hair
Was certain to fix the public stare,
And the constant cry was, 'I declare!'
And 'Did you ever!' and 'Just look there!'
Among the dazzled girls.

XII.

Now Captain Jones was a master bold
Of a merchant ship some dozen years old,
And every name could have easily told,
(And never confound the 'hull' and the 'hold,')
Throughout her inventory;
And he had travelled in foreign parts,
And learned a number of foreign arts,
And played the deuse with foreign hearts,
As the Captain told the story.

XIII.

He had learned to chatter the French and Spanish,
To splutter the Dutch, and mutter the Danish,
In a way that sounded oracular;
Had gabbled among the Portuguese,
And caught the Tartar, or rather a piece
Of 'broken China,' it wasn't Chinese,
Any more than his own vernacular!

XIV.

How Captain Jones was wont to shine
In the line of ships! (not Ships of the Line,)
How he'd brag of the water over his wine,
And of women over the water!

And then, if you credit the Captain's phrase,
He was more expert in such queer ways
As 'doubling capes' and 'putting in stays,'
Than any milliner's daughter!

XV.

Now the Captain kept in constant pay
A single Mate, as a Captain may,
(In a nautical, not in a naughty way,
As 'mates' are sometimes carried;)
But to hear him prose of the squalls that arose
In the dead of the night to break his repose;
Of white-caps and cradles, and such things as those
And of breezes that ended in regular blows,
You'd have sworn the Captain was married!

XVI.

The Captain's morals were fair enough,
Though a sailor's life is rather rough,
By dint of the ocean's force;
And that one who makes so many, in ships,
Should make, upon shore, occasional 'trips,'
Seems quite a matter of course.

XVII.

And Captain Jones was stiff as a post
To the vulgar fry, but among the most
Genteel and polished, ruled the roast,
As no professional cook could boast
    That ever you set your eye on;
Indeed, 'twas enough to make him vain,
For the pretty and proud confessed his reign,
And Captain Jones, in manners and mane,
    Was deemed a genuine lion.

XVIII.

And the Captain revelled early and late,
At the balls and routs of the rich and great,
And seemed the veriest child of *fêtes*,
    Though merely a minion of pleasure;
And he laughed with the girls in merry sport,
And paid the mammas the civilest court,
And drank their wine, whatever the sort,
By the nautical rule of 'Any port ——'
    You may add the rest at leisure.

XIX.

Miss Susan Brown was a dashing girl
As ever revolved in the waltz's whirl,
Or twinkled a foot in the polka's twirl,
    By the glare of spermaceti;

And SUSAN'S form was trim and slight,
And her beautiful skin, as if in spite
Of her dingy name, was exceedingly white,
And her azure eyes were 'sparkling and bright,'
    And so was her favorite ditty.

XX.

And SUSAN BROWN had a score of names,
Like the very voluminous Mr. JAMES,
(Who got at the Font his strongest claims
    To be reckoned a Man of Letters;)
But thinking the task will hardly please
Scholars who've taken the higher degrees,
To be set repeating their A, B, C's,
I choose to reject such fetters as these,
    Though merely Nominal fetters.

XXI.

The patronymical name of the maid
Was so completely overlaid
    With a long prænominal cover,
That if each additional proper noun
Was laid with additional emphasis down,
Miss SUSAN was done uncommonly BROWN,
    The moment her christ'ning was over!

XXII.

And SUSAN was versed in modern romance,
In the Modes of MURRAY and Modes of France,
And had learned to sing and learned to dance,
In a style decidedly pretty;
And SUSAN was versed in classical lore,
In the works of HORACE, and several more
Whose *opera* now would be voted a bore
By the lovers of DONIZETTI.

XXIII.

And SUSAN was rich. Her provident sire
Had piled the dollars up higher and higher,
By dint of his personal labors,
Till he reckoned at last a sufficient amount
To be counted, himself, a man of account
Among his affluent neighbors.

XXIV.

By force of careful culture alone,
Old BROWN'S estate had rapidly grown
A plum for his only daughter;
And after all the fanciful dreams
Of golden fountains and golden streams,
The sweat of patient labor seems
The true Pactolian water.

XXV.

And while your theorist worries his mind
In hopes 'the magical stone' to find,
By some alchemical gammon,
Practical people, by regular knocks,
Are filling their 'pockets full of rocks'
From the golden mountain of Mammon!

XXVI.

With charms like these, you may well suppose
Miss SUSAN BROWN had plenty of beaux,
Breathing nothing but passion;
And twenty sought her hand to gain,
And twenty sought her hand in vain,
Were 'cut,' and didn't 'come again,'
In the Ordinary fashion.

XXVII.

Captain JONES, by the common voice,
At length was voted the man of her choice,
And she his favorite fair;
It wasn't the Captain's manly face,
His native sense, nor foreign grace,
That took her heart from its proper place
And put it into a tenderer case,
But his beautiful coal-black hair!

XXVIII.

How it is, *why* it is, none can tell,
But all philosophers know full well,
Though puzzled about the action,
That of all the forces under the sun
You can hardly find a stronger one
Than capillary attraction.

XXIX.

The locks of canals are strong as rocks;
And wedlock is strong as a banker's box;
And there's strength in the locks a Cockney cocks
At innocent birds, to give himself knocks;
In the locks of safes, and those safety-locks,
They call the Permutation;
But of all the locks that ever were made
In Nature's shops, or the shops of trade,
The subtlest combination
Of beauty and strength is found in those
Which grace the heads of belles and beaux
In every civilized nation!

XXX.

The gossips whispered it through the town,
That 'Captain JONES loved SUSAN BROWN;'
But, speaking with due precision,

The gossips' tattle was out of joint,
For the lady's 'blunt' was the only point
That dazzled the lover's vision!

XXXI.

And the Captain begged, in his smoothest tones,
Miss SUSAN BROWN to be Mistress JONES, —
Flesh of his flesh and bone of his bones,
Till death the union should sever;
For these are the words employed, of course,
Though Death is cheated, sometimes, by Divorce;
A fact which gives an equivocal force
To that beautiful phrase, 'forever!'

XXXII.

And SUSAN sighed the conventional 'Nay'
In such a bewitching, affirmative way,
The Captain perceived 'twas the feminine 'Ay,'
And sealed it in such commotion,
That no 'lip-service' that ever was paid
To the ear of a god, or the cheek of a maid,
Looked more like real devotion!

XXXIII.

And SUSAN's Mamma made an elegant *fête*,
And exhibited all the family plate
In honor of SUSAN's lover;

For now 'twas settled, another trip
Over the sea in his merchant ship
And his bachelor-ship was over.

XXXIV.

There was an Alderman, well-to-do,
Who was fond of talking about *vertù*,
And had, besides, the genuine *goût*,
If one might credit his telling;
And the boast was true beyond a doubt,
If he had only pronounced it 'gout,'
According to English spelling!

XXXV.

A crockery-merchant of great parade,
Always boasting of having made
His large estate in the China trade;
Several affluent tanners;
A lawyer, whose most important 'case'
Was that which kept his books in place;
His wife, a lady of matchless grace,
Who bought her form, and made her face,
Who plainly borrowed her manners;

XXXVI.

A druggist; an undevout divine;
A banker, who'd got as rich as a mine
'In the cotton trade and sugar line,'

Along the Atlantic border;
A doctor, fumbling his golden seals;
And an undertaker close at his heels,
Quite in the natural order!

XXXVII.

People of rank, and people of wealth,
Plethoric people in delicate health,
(Who fast in public, and feast by stealth,)
And people slender and hearty,
Flocked in so fast, 'twas plain to the eye
Of any observer standing by,
That party-spirit was running high,
And this was the popular party!

XXXVIII.

To tell what griefs and woes betide
The hapless world, from female pride,
Were a long and dismal story;
Alas! for SUSAN and womankind!
A sudden ambition seized her mind,
In the height of her party-glory.

XXXIX.

To pique a group of laughing girls
Who stood admiring the Captain's curls,

She formed the resolution
To get a lock of her lover's hair,
In the gaze of the guests assembled there,
By some expedient, foul or fair,
Before the party's conclusion.

XL.

'Only a lock, dear Captain! — no more,
"A lock for memory," I implore!'
But JONES, the gayest of quizzers,
Replied, as he gave his eye a cock,
''Tis a treacherous memory needs a lock,'
And dodged the envious scissors.

XLI.

Alas! that SUSAN couldn't refrain,
In her zeal the precious lock to gain,
From laying her hand on the lion's mane!
To see the cruel mocking,
And hear the short, affected cough,
The general titter, and chuckle, and scoff,
When the Captain's Patent Wig came off,
Was really dreadfully shocking!

XLII.

Of SUSAN's swoon, the tale is told
That long before her earthly mould
Regained its ghostly tenant,
Her luckless, wigless, loveless lover,
Was on the sea, and 'half-seas-over,'
Dreaming that some piratical rover
Had carried away his Pennant!

A RHYMED EPISTLE

TO THE EDITOR OF THE KNICKERBOCKER MAGAZINE.

Dear Knick: While myself and my spouse
  Sat tea-ing last evening, and chatting,
And, mindful of conjugal vows,
  Were nicely agreed in combating,
It chanced that myself and my wife
  ('Twas Madam occasioned the pother!)
Falling suddenly into a strife,
  Came near falling out with each other!

In a brisk, miscellaneous chat,
  Quite in tune with the chime of the tea-things,
We were talking of this and of that,
  Just as each of us happened to see things,
When some how or other it chanced
  (I don't quite remember the cue,)
That as talking and tea-ing advanced,
  We found we were talking of you!

I think, — but perhaps I am wrong,
  Such a subtle old chap is Suggestion,
As he forces each topic along
  By the trick of the 'previous question,'
Some remarks on a bacchanal revel
  Suggested that horrible elf
With the hoof and the horns, — and the Devil,
  Excuse me, suggested yourself!

'Ah! Knick, to be sure; by the way,'
  Quoth Madam, 'what sort of a man
Do you take him to be! — nay, but stay,
  And let *me* guess him out if I can.
He's young, and quite handsome, no doubt;
  Rather slender, and not over-tall;
And he loves a snug little turn-out,
  And turns out "quite a love" at a ball!'

And then she went on to portray
  Such a very delightful ideal,
That a sensible stranger would say
  It really couldn't be real.
'And his wife, what a lady must *she* be?
  (Knick's married, that *I* know, and *you* know;)
You'll find her a delicate Hebe,
  And not your magnificent Juno!'

Now I am a man, you must learn,
  Less famous for beauty than strength,
And for aught I could ever discern,
  Of rather superfluous length.
In truth, 'tis but seldom one meets
  Such a Titan in human abodes,
And when I stalk over the streets,
  I'm a perfect Colossus of roads!

So I frowned like a Tragedy-Roman,
  For in painting the beautiful elf
As the form of your lady, the woman
  Took care to be drawing herself;
While, mark you, the picture she drew
  So deused *con amore* and free,
That fanciful likeness of you,
  Was by no means a portrait of me!

'How lucky for ladies,' I hinted,
  'That in our republican land
They may prattle, without being stinted,
  Of matters they don't understand;
I'll show you, dear Madam, that "KNICK"
  Isn't dapper nor daintily slim,
But a gentleman decently thick,
  With a manly extension of limb.'

'And as to his youth — talk of flowers
  Blooming gayly in frosty December!
I'll warrant, his juvenile hours
  Are things he can scarcely remember!
Here, Madam, quite plain to be seen,
  Is the chap you would choose for a lover!'
And producing your own Magazine,
  I pointed elate to the cover!

'You see, ma'am, 'tis just as I said,
  His locks are as gray as a rat;
Here, look at the crown of his head,
  'Tis bald as the crown of my hat!'
'Nay, my dear,' interrupted my wife,
  Who began to be casting about
To get the last word in the strife,
  ''T is his grandfather's picture, no doubt!'

THE DOG DAYS.

'Hot!—hot!—all piping hot!"—*City Cries.*

Heaven help us all in these terrific days!
  The burning sun upon the earth is pelting
With his directest, fiercest, hottest rays,
  And every thing is melting!

Fat men, infatuate, fan the stagnant air,
  In rash essay to cool their inward glowing,
While with each stroke, in dolorous despair,
  They feel the fever growing!

The lean and lathy find a fate as hard,
  For, all a-dry, they burn like any tinder
Beneath the solar blaze, till withered, charred
  And crisped away to cinder!

E'en Stoics now are in the melting mood,
  And vestal cheeks are most unseemly florid;
The very zone that girts the frigid prude,
  Is now intensely torrid!

The dogs lie lolling in the deepest shade;
  The pigs are all a-wallow in the gutters,
And not a household creature — cat or maid,
  But querulously mutters!

''Tis dreadful, dreadful hot!' exclaims each one
  Unto his sweating, sweltering, roasting neighbor,
Then mops his brow, and sighs, as he had done
  A quite herculean labor!

And friends who pass each other in the town,
  Say no good morrows when they come together,
But only mutter, with a dismal frown,
  'What horrid, horrid weather!'

While prudent mortals curb with strictest care
  All vagrant curs, it seems the queerest puzzle
The Dog-star rages rabid through the air,
  Without the slightest muzzle!

But Jove is wise and equal in his sway,
  Howe'er it seems to clash with human reason,
His fiery dogs will soon have had their day,
  And men shall have a season!

ON A RECENT CLASSIC CONTROVERSY.

AN EPIGRAM.

NAY, marvel not to see these scholars fight,
  In brave disdain of certain scath and scar;
'Tis but the genuine, old, Hellenic spite,—
  'When Greek meets Greek, then comes the tug of
      war!'

ANOTHER.

QUOTH David to Daniel—'Why is it these scholars
  Abuse one another whenever they speak?'
Quoth Daniel to David—'It nat'rally follers
  Folks come to hard words if they meddle with
      Greek!'

THE GHOST-PLAYER.

A BALLAD.

Tom Goodwin was an actor-man,
Old Drury's pride and boast
In all the light and sprite-ly parts,
Especially the Ghost.

Now Tom was very fond of drink,
Of almost every sort,
Comparative and positive,
From porter up to port.

But grog, like grief, is fatal stuff
For any man to sup;
For when it fails to pull him down,
It's sure to blow him up.

And so it fared with ghostly Tom,
  Who day by day was seen
A-swelling, till (as lawyers say)
  He fairly lost his lean.

At length the manager observed
  He'd better leave his post,
And said, he played the very deuse
  Whene'er he played the Ghost.

'Twas only 'tother night he saw
  A fellow swing his hat,
And heard him cry, 'By all the gods!
  The Ghost is getting fat!'

'Twould never do, the case was plain;
  His eyes he couldn't shut;
Ghosts shouldn't make the people laugh,
  And Tom was quite a *butt*.

Tom's actor friends said ne'er a word
  To cheer his drooping heart;
Though more than one was burning up
  With zeal to 'take his part.'

Tom argued very plausibly ;
He said he didn't doubt
That Hamlet's father drank and grew,
In years, a little stout.

And so, 'twas natural, he said,
And quite a proper plan,
To have his spirit represent
A portly sort of man.

'Twas all in vain ; the manager
Said he was not in sport,
And, like a gen'ral, bade poor Tom
Surrender up his *forte.*

He'd do perhaps in heavy parts ,
Might answer for a monk,
Or porter to the elephant,
To carry round his trunk ;

But in the Ghost his day was past —
He'd never do for that ;
A Ghost might just as well be dead
As plethoric and fat !

Alas! next day poor Tom was found
  As stiff as any post—
For he had lost his character,
  And given up the Ghost!

ON AN ILL-READ LAWYER.

AN EPIGRAM.

An idle attorney besought a brother
For 'something to read—some novel or other,
    That was really fresh and new.'
'Take Chitty!' replied his legal friend,
'There isn't a book that I could lend
    Would prove more "novel" to you!'

A BENEDICT'S APPEAL TO A BACHELOR.

'Double! double!' — *Shakspeare.*

1.

DEAR CHARLES, be persuaded to wed,
For a sensible fellow like you,
It's high time to think of a bed,
And muffins and coffee for two!
So have done with your doubt and delaying, —
With a soul so adapted to mingle,
No wonder the neighbors are saying
'Tis singular you should be single!

2.

Don't say that you have'nt got time, —
That business demands your attention, —
There's not the least reason nor rhyme
In the wisest excuse you can mention.

Don't tell me about 'other fish,'—
  Your duty is done when you buy 'em,—
And you never will relish the dish,
  Unless you've a woman to fry 'em!

3.

Don't listen to querulous stories
  By desperate damsels related,
Who sneer at connubial glories,
  Because they've known couples mismated.
Such people, if they had their pleasure,
  Because silly bargains are made,
Would deem it a rational measure
  To lay an embargo on trade!

4.

You may dream of poetical fame,
  But your wishes may chance to miscarry,—
The best way of sending one's name
  To posterity, Charles, is to marry!
And here I am willing to own,
  After soberly thinking upon it,
I'd very much rather be known
  For a beautiful son, than a sonnet!

5.

To Procrastination be deaf, —
(A homily sent from above,)
The scoundrel's not only 'the thief
Of time,' but of beauty and love!
O delay not one moment to win
A prize that is truly worth winning, —
Celibacy, Charles, is a sin,
And sadly prolific of sinning!

6.

Then pray bid your doubting good by,
And dismiss all fantastic alarms, —
I'll be sworn you've a girl in your eye
'Tis your duty to have in your arms!
Some trim little maiden of twenty,
A beautiful, azure-eyed elf,
With virtues and graces in plenty,
And no failing but loving yourself!

7.

Don't search for 'an angel' a minute;
For granting you win in the sequel,
The deuse, after all, would be in it,
With a union so very unequal!

The angels, it must be confessed,
  In *this* world are rather uncommon;
And allow me, dear Charles, to suggest
  You'll be better content with a woman!

8.

I could furnish a bushel of reasons
  For choosing a conjugal mate, —
It agrees with all climates and seasons,
  And gives you a 'double estate!'
To one's parents 'tis (gratefully) due, —
  Just think what a terrible thing
'Twould have been, sir, for me and for you,
  If *ours* had forgotten the ring!

9.

Then there's the economy — clear,
  By poetical algebra shown, —
If your wife has a grief or a fear,
  One half, by the law, is your own!
And as to the joys — by division,
  They're nearly quadrupled, 'tis said,
(Though I never could see the addition
  Quite plain in the item of bread).

10.

Remember, I do not pretend
  There's any thing 'perfect' about it,
But this I'll aver to the end,
  Life's very imperfect without it!
'Tis not that there's 'poetry' in it, —
  As, doubtless, there may be to those
Endowed with a genius to win it, —
  But I'll warrant you excellent prose!

11.

Then, Charles, be persuaded to wed, —
  For a sensible fellow like you,
It's high time to think of a bed,
  And muffins and coffee for two;
So have done with your doubt and delaying, —
  With a soul so adapted to mingle,
No wonder the neighbors are saying
  'Tis singular you should be single!

BOYS.

'The proper study of mankind is man,' —
The most perplexing one, no doubt, is woman;
The subtlest study that the mind can scan,
Of all deep problems, heavenly or human!

But of all studies in the round of learning,
From nature's marvels down to human toys,
To minds well fitted for acute discerning,
The very queerest one is that of boys!

If to ask questions that would puzzle Plato,
And all the schoolmen of the middle age, —
If to make precepts worthy of old Cato,
Be deemed philosophy, — your boy's a sage!

If the possession of a teeming fancy, —
(Although, forsooth, the younker doesn't know it,)
Which he can use in rarest necromancy,
Be thought poetical, your boy's a poet!

If a strong will and most courageous bearing,
  If to be cruel as the Roman Nero ;
If all that's chivalrous, and all that's daring,
  Can make a hero, then the boy's a hero !

But changing soon with his increasing stature,
  The boy is lost in manhood's riper age,
And with him goes his former triple nature, —
  No longer Poet, Hero, now, nor Sage !

WOMAN'S WILL.

AN EPIGRAM.

MEN dying make their wills, — but wives
    Escape a work so sad ;
Why should they make what all their lives
    The gentle dames have had ?

THE COLD WATER-MAN.

A BALLAD.

It was an honest fisherman,
  I knew him passing well, —
And he lived by a little pond,
  Within a little dell.

A grave and quiet man was he,
  Who loved his hook and rod, —
So even ran his line of life,
  His neighbors thought it odd.

For science and for books, he said
  He never had a wish, —
No school to him was worth a fig,
  Except a school of fish.

He ne'er aspired to rank or wealth,
  Nor cared about a name, —
For though much famed for fish was he,
  He never fished for fame!

Let others bend their necks at sight
  Of Fashion's gilded wheels,
He ne'er had learned the art to 'bob'
  For any thing but eels!

A cunning fisherman was he,
  His angles all were right;
The smallest nibble at his bait
  Was sure to prove 'a bite!'

All day this fisherman would sit
  Upon an ancient log,
And gaze into the water, like
  Some sedentary frog;

With all the seeming innocence,
  And that unconscious look,
That other people often wear
  When they intend to 'hook!'

To charm the fish he never spoke, —
  Although his voice was fine,
He found the most convenient way
  Was just to drop a line!

And many a gudgeon of the pond,
  If they could speak to-day,
Would own, with grief, this angler had
  A mighty taking way!

Alas! one day this fisherman
  Had taken too much grog,
And being but a landsman, too,
  He couldn't keep the log!

'Twas all in vain with might and main
  He strove to reach the shore —
Down — down he went, to feed the fish
  He'd baited oft before!

The jury gave their verdict that
  'Twas nothing else but gin
Had caused the fisherman to be
  So sadly taken in;

Though one stood out upon a whim,
And said the angler's slaughter,
To be exact about the fact,
Was, clearly, gin-and-*water !*

The moral of this mournful tale.
To all is plain and clear, —
That drinking habits bring a man
Too often to his bier;

And he who scorns to 'take the pledge,'
And keep the promise fast,
May be, in spite of fate, a *stiff*
Cold water-man at last !

ON AN UGLY PERSON SITTING FOR A DAGUERREOTYPE.

AN EPIGRAM.

Here Nature in her glass, — the wanton elf, —
Sits gravely making faces at herself;
And while she scans each clumsy feature o'er,
Repeats the blunders that she made before !

A COLLEGE REMINISCENCE.

(ADDRESSED TO THOMAS B. THORPE, ESQ. OF NEW ORLEANS.)

DEAR TOM, have you forgot the day
When, long ago, we used to stray
        Among the 'Haddams?'
Where, in the mucky road, a man
(The road was built on Adam's plan,
        And not McAdam's!)

Went down — down — down, one stormy night,
And disappeared from human sight,
        All save his hat, —
Which raised in sober minds a sense
Of some mysterious Providence
        In sparing that?

I think 'twill please you, Tom, to hear
The man who in that night of fear
Went down terrestrial,
Worked out a passage like a miner,
And pricking through somewhere in China,
Came up Celestial!

Ah! those were memorable times,
And worth embalming in my rhymes,
When, at the summons
Of chapel bell, we left our sport
For lessons most uncommon short,
Or shorter commons!

I mind me, Tom, you often drew
Nice portraits, and exceeding true,—
To your intention!
The most impracticable faces
Discovered unsuspected graces,
By your invention.

On brainless heads the finest bumps
(Erected by your pencil-thumps,)
Were plainly seen;
Your Yankees all were very Greek,
Unchosen aunts grew 'choice antique,'
And blues turned green!

The swarthy suddenly were fair,
And yellow changed to auburn hair
Or sunny flax;
And people very thin and flat,
Like Aldermen, grew round and fat
On canvas-backs!

I well remember all your art
To make the best of every part, —
I am certain *no* man
Could better coax a wrinkle out,
Or elevate a lowly snout,
Or snub a Roman!

Young gentlemen with leaden eyes
Stared wildly out on lowering skies,
Quite Corsair-fashion;
And greenish orbs got very blue,
And linsey-woolsey maidens grew
Almost Circassian!

And many an ancient maiden aunt
As lean and lank as John O'Gaunt,
Or even lanker,
By art transformed and newly drest
Could boast for once as full a chest
As — any banker!

Ah! we were jolly youngsters then,
But now we're sober-sided men,
Half through life's journey;
And you've turned author, Tom, I hear,—
And I,—you'll think it very queer,—
Have turned attorney!

Heaven bless you, Tom, in house and heart!
(That we should live so far apart,
Is much a pity,)
And may you multiply your name,
And have a very 'crescent' fame,
Just like your city!

FAMILY QUARRELS.

AN EPIGRAM.

'A fool,' said Jeanette, 'is a creature I hate!'
'But hating,' quoth John, 'is immoral;
Besides, my dear girl, it's a terrible fate
To be found in a family quarrel!'

SONNET TO A CLAM.

Dum tacent *clamant*.

INGLORIOUS FRIEND! most confident I am
  Thy life is one of very little ease;
  Albeit men mock thee with their similes
And prate of being 'happy as a clam!'
What though thy shell protects thy fragile head
  From the sharp bailiffs of the briny sea?
  Thy valves are, sure, no safety-valves to thee,
While rakes are free to desecrate thy bed,
And bear thee off, — as foemen take their spoil, —
  Far from thy friends and family to roam;
  Forced, like a Hessian, from thy native home,
To meet destruction in a foreign broil!
  Though thou art tender, yet thy humble bard
  Declares, O clam! thy case is shocking hard!

A REASONABLE PETITION.

You say, dearest girl, you esteem me,
And hint of respectful regard,
And I'm certain it wouldn't beseem me
Such an excellent gift to discard.
But even the Graces, you'll own,
Would lose half their beauty, apart, —
And Esteem, when she stands all alone,
Looks most unbecomingly tart.
So grant me, dear girl, this petition: —
If Esteem e'er again should come hither,
Just to keep her in cheerful condition,
Let Love come in company with her!

GUNEOPATHY.

I SAW a lady yesterday,
  A regular M. D.,
Who'd taken from the Faculty
  Her medical degree;
And I thought if ever I was sick,
  My doctor she should be!

I pity the deluded man
  Who foolishly consults
Another man, in hopes to find
  Such magical results
As when a pretty woman lays
  Her hand upon his pulse!

I had a strange disorder once,
  A kind of chronic chill

That all the doctors in the town,
  With all their vaunted skill,
Could never cure, I'm very sure,
  With powder nor with pill;

I don't know what they called it
  In their pompous terms of Art,
Nor if they thought it mortal
  In such a vital part,—
I only know 'twas reckoned
  'Something icy round the heart!'

A lady came—her presence brought
  The blood into my ears!
She took my hand—and something like
  A fever now appears!
Great Galen!—I was all aglow,
  Though I'd been cold for years!

Perhaps it is'nt every case
  That's fairly in her reach,
But should I e'er be ill again,
  I fervently beseech
That I may have, for life or death,
  A lady for my 'leech!'

A PHILOSOPHICAL QUERY.

TO ———

If Virtue be measured by what we resist,
  When against Inclination we strive,
You and I have been proved, we may fairly insist,
  The most virtuous mortals alive!
Now Virtue, we know, is the brightest of pearls,
  But as Pleasure is hard of evasion,
Should we envy, or pity, the stoical churls
  Who never have known a temptation?

COMIC MISERIES.

1.

My dear young friend, whose shining wit
  Sets all the room ablaze,
Don't think yourself 'a happy dog,'
  For all your merry ways;
But learn to wear a sober phiz,
  Be stupid, if you can,
It's such a very serious thing
  To be a funny man!

2.

You're at an evening party, with
  A group of pleasant folks, —
You venture quietly to crack
  The least of little jokes, —

A lady doesn't catch the point,
  And begs you to explain —
Alas! for one who drops a jest
  And takes it up again!

3.

You're talking deep philosophy
  With very special force,
To edify a clergyman
  With suitable discourse, —
You think you've got him — when he calls
  A friend across the way,
And begs you'll say that funny thing
  You said the other day!

4.

You drop a pretty *jeu-de-mot*
  Into a neighbor's ears,
Who likes to give you credit for
  The clever thing he hears,
And so he hawks your jest about,
  The old, authentic one,
Just breaking off the point of it,
  And leaving out the pun!

5.

By sudden change in politics,
  Or sadder change in Polly,
You, lose your love, or loaves, and fall
  A prey to melancholy,
While every body marvels why
  Your mirth is under ban, —
They think your very grief 'a joke,'
  You're such a funny man!

6.

You follow up a stylish card
  That bids you come and dine,
And bring along your freshest wit,
  (To pay for musty wine,)
You're looking very dismal, when
  My lady bounces in,
And wonders what you're thinking of,
  And why you don't begin!

7.

You're telling to a knot of friends
  A fancy-tale of woes
That cloud your matrimonial sky,
  And banish all repose, —

A solemn lady overhears
  The story of your strife,
And tells the town the pleasant news: —
  You quarrel with your wife!

8.

My dear young friend, whose shining wit
  Sets all the room ablaze,
Don't think yourself 'a happy dog,'
  For all your merry ways;
But learn to wear a sober phiz,
  Be stupid, if you can,
It's such a very serious thing
  To be a funny man!

THE OLD CHAPEL-BELL.

A BALLAD.[1]

WITHIN a churchyard's sacred ground,
  Whose fading tablets tell
Where they who built the village church
  In solemn silence dwell,
Half-hidden in the earth, there lies
  An ancient Chapel-Bell.

Broken, decayed and covered o'er
  With mouldering leaves and rust;
Its very name and date concealed
  Beneath a cankering crust;
Forgotten — like its early friends,
  Who sleep in neighboring dust.

---

[1] This ballad is a paraphrase of a beautiful prose tale written by Mrs. ALICE B. NEAL, and published anonymously, several years ago, as a translation 'from the German.' The story is so exceedingly *Germanesque* in its style and spirit, that the best scholars in the country did not suspect its American origin, until the fact was recently disclosed by the gifted authoress.

Yet it was once a trusty Bell,
  Of most sonorous lung,
And many a joyous wedding peal,
  And many a knell had rung,
Ere Time had cracked its brazen sides,
  And broke its iron tongue.

And many a youthful heart had danced
  In merry Christmas-time,
To hear its pleasant roundelay,
  Sung out in ringing rhyme;
And many a worldly thought been checked
  To list its Sabbath chime.

A youth — a bright and happy boy,
  One sultry summer's day,
Aweary of his bat and ball,
  Chanced hitherward to stray,
To read a little book he had
  And rest him from his play.

'A soft and shady spot is this!'
  The rosy youngster cried,
And sat him down, beneath a tree,
  That ancient Bell beside;
(But, hidden in the tangled grass,
  The Bell he ne'er espied.)

Anon, a mist fell on his book,
  The letters seemed to stir,
And though, full oft, his flagging sight
  The boy essayed to spur,
The mazy page was quickly lost
  Beneath a cloudy blur.

And while he marvelled much at this,
  And wondered how it came,
He felt a languor creeping o'er
  His young and weary frame,
And heard a voice, a gentle voice,
  That plainly spoke his name.

That gentle voice that named his name,
  Entranced him like a spell,
Upon his ear, so very near
  And suddenly it fell;
Yet soft and musical, as 'twere
  The whisper of a bell.

'Since last I spoke,' the voice began,—
  'Seems many a dreary year!
(Albeit, 'tis only since thy birth
  I've lain neglected here)
Pray list, while I rehearse a tale
  Behooves thee much to hear.

'Once, from yon ivied tower, I watched
  The villagers, around,
And gave to all their joys and griefs
  A sympathetic sound, —
But most are sleeping, now, within
  This consecrated ground.

'I used to ring my merriest peal
  To hail the blushing bride;
I sadly tolled for men cut down
  In strength and manly pride;
And solemnly, — not mournfully, —
  When little children died.

'But, chief, my duty was to bid
  The villagers repair,
On each returning Sabbath morn,
  Unto the House of Prayer,
And in his own appointed place,
  The Savior's mercy share.

'Ah! well I mind me of a child,
  A gleesome, happy maid,
Who came with constant step, to church
  In comely garb arrayed,
And knelt her down full solemnly,
  And penitently prayed.

'And oft, when church was done, I marked
  That little maiden near
This pleasant spot, with book in hand,
  As you are sitting here, —
She read the Story of the Cross,
  And wept with grief sincere.

'Years rolled away, — and I beheld
  The child to woman grown;
Her cheek was fairer, and her eye
  With brighter lustre shone;
But childhood's truth and innocence
  Were still the maiden's own.

'I never rang a merrier peal,
  Than when, a joyous bride,
She stood beneath the sacred porch,
  A noble youth beside,
And plighted him her maiden troth,
  In maiden love and pride.

'I never tolled a deeper knell,
  Than when, in after years,
They laid her in the churchyard here,
  Where this low mound appears —
(The very grave, my boy, that you
  Are watering now with tears!)

'*It is thy mother!* gentle boy,
That claims this tale of mine —
Thou art a flower whose fatal birth
Destroyed the parent vine!
A precious flower art thou, my child, —
TWO LIVES WERE GIVEN FOR THINE!

'One was thy sainted mother's, when
She gave thee mortal birth;
And one thy Savior's, when in death,
He shook the solid earth;
Go! boy, and live as may befit
Thy life's exceeding worth!'

The boy awoke, as from a dream,
And, thoughtful, looked around,
But nothing saw save at his feet,
His mother's lowly mound,
And by its side that ancient Bell
Half-hidden in the ground!

THE LADY ANN.

A BALLAD.

'SHE'LL soon be here, the Lady ANN,'
  The children cried in glee;
'She always comes at four o'clock,
  And now it's striking three.'

At stroke of four the lady came,
  A lady passing fair;
And she sat and gazed adown the road,
  With a long and eager stare.

'The mail! the mail!' the idlers cried,
  At sight of a coach-and-four;
'The mail! the mail!' and at the word,
  The coach was at the door.

Up sprang in haste the Lady Ann,
  And marked with anxious eye
The travellers, who, one by one,
  Were slowly passing by.

'Alack! alack!' the lady cried,
  'He surely named to-day;
He'll come to-morrow, then,' she sighed,
  And turning, strolled away.

''Tis passing odd, upon my word,'
  The landlord now began;
'A strange romance! — that woman, Sirs,
  Is called The Lady Ann.

'She dwells hard by upon the hill,
  The widow of Sir John,
Who died abroad, come August next,
  Just twenty years agone.

'A hearty neighbor, Sirs, was he,
  A bold, true-hearted man;
And a fonder pair were seldom seen,
  Than he and Lady Ann.

'They scarce had been a twelvemonth wed,
  When! — ill betide the day! —
Sir John was called to go in haste
  Some hundred miles away.

'Ne'er lovers in the fairy tales
  A truer love could boast;
And many were the gentle words
  That came and went by post.

'A month or more had passed away,
  When by the post came down
The joyous news that such a day
  Sir John would be in town.

'Full gleesome was the Lady Ann
  To read the welcome word,
And promptly at the hour she came,
  To meet her wedded lord.

'Alas! alas! he came not back!
  There only came instead,
A mournful message by the post,
  That good Sir John was dead!

'One piercing shriek, and Lady Ann
  Had swooned upon the floor;
Good Sirs, it was a fearful grief
  That gentle lady bore!

'We raised her up; her ebbing life
  Began again to dawn;
She muttered wildly to herself,—
  'Twas plain her wits were gone.

'A strange forgetfulness came o'er
  Her sad, bewildered mind,
And to the grief that drove her mad
  Her memory was blind!

'Ah! since that hour she little wots
  Full twenty years are fled!
She little wots, poor Lady Ann!
  Her wedded lord is dead.

'But each returning day she deems
  The day he fixed to come;
And ever at the wonted hour
  She's here to greet him home.

‘ And when the coach is at the door,
  She marks with eager eye
The travellers, as one by one
  They're slowly passing by.

‘ “ Alack ! ” she cries, in plaintive tone,
  “ He surely named to-day !
He'll come to-morrow, then,” she sighs,
  And turning, strolls away.’

GIRLHOOD.

WITH rosy cheeks, and merry-dancing curls,
    And eyes of tender light,
O, very beautiful are little girls,
    And goodly to the sight!

Here comes a group to seek my lonely bower,
    Ere waning Autumn dies, —
How like the dew-drops on a drooping flower,
    Are smiles from gentle eyes!

What beaming gladness lights each fairy face
    The while the elves advance,
Now speeding swiftly in a gleesome race,
    Now whirling in a dance!

What heavenly pleasure o'er the spirit rolls,
When all the air along
Floats the sweet music of untainted souls,
In bright, unsullied song!

The sacred nymphs that guard this sylvan ground
May sport unseen with these,
And joy to hear their ringing laugh resound
Among the clustering trees!

With rosy cheeks, and merry-dancing curls,
And eyes of tender light,
O, very beautiful are little girls,
And goodly to the sight!

BEREAVEMENT.

A SONNET.

Nay, weep not, dearest, though the child be dead,
He lives again in Heaven's unclouded life,
With other angels that have early fled
From these dark scenes of sorrow, sin, and strife;
Nay, weep not, dearest, though thy yearning love
Would fondly keep for earth its fairest flowers,
And e'en deny to brighter realms above
The few that deck this dreary world of ours:
Though much it seems a wonder and a woe
That one so loved should be so early lost,
And hallowed tears may unforbidden flow
To mourn the blossom that we cherished most —
Yet all is well; God's good design I see,
That where our treasure is, our hearts may be!

MY BOYHOOD.

Ah me! those joyous days are gone!
I little dreamt, till they were flown,
How fleeting were the hours!
For, lest he break the pleasing spell,
Time bears for youth a muffled bell,
And hides his face in flowers!

Ah! well I mind me of the days,
Still bright in memory's flattering rays,
When all was fair and new;
When knaves were only found in books,
And friends were known by friendly looks,
And love was always true!

While yet of sin I scarcely dreamed,
And every thing was what it seemed,
　　And all too bright for choice ;
When fays were wont to guard my sleep,
And *Crusoe* still could make me weep,
　　And *Santaclaus*, rejoice !

When Heaven was pictured to my thought,
(In spite of all my mother taught
　　Of happiness serene)
A theatre of boyish plays —
One glorious round of holidays,
　　Without a school between !

Ah me ! those joyous days are gone ;
I little dreamt, till they were flown,
　　How fleeting were the hours !
For, lest he break the pleasing spell,
Time bears for youth a muffled bell,
　　And hides his face in flowers !

THE TIMES.

THE TIMES:

A POEM READ BEFORE THE BOSTON MERCANTILE LIBRARY ASSOCIATION, NOVEMBER 14, 1849.

THE Muses once, — so sacred myths declare, —
(See classic Keightly, Cruzer, or Lempriere,)
On cleft Parnassus held a lofty seat,
Where, in the quiet of their calm retreat,
With sweet accord they spent the rosy hours,
And wove bright garlands of perennial flowers;
Nine blooming sisters, each with separate aim,
Yet all rejoicing in the common fame,
Alone attentive to their high behests,
No jealous cares disturbed their tender breasts,
For Phœbus, watchful of the sacred Nine,
Warned off intruders with a magic sign! —
You've seen the like in Lowell mills, where scores,
In gold or ochre, guard the inner doors;
A frequent sight in any factory town,
Where idle cit, or curious country clown,

Reads, at a glance, in letters large and clear,
The startling caution — 'No admittance here!'
 What amorous bard, the hidden Nine to view, —
First scaled the wall, or forced a passage through, —
What 'gay Lothario' found at length a way
To win the maids and lead them all astray,
Is yet unknown — this only can be told,
Some curst intruder broke Apollo's fold,
And all-remorseless for the grave abuse,
In Phœbus' spite let all the Muses loose!
Far from their old Parnassian groves to roam, —
To grace, instead, some airy garret-home,
(Where, free from bailiffs, poetasters rhyme,
And, thankless, waste their tapers and their time,
While through the night they fondly toil for nought,
Angling in ink-stands for some gudgeon-thought).
Nor this the worst that sprang from such a cause.
Released at once from chaste Diana's laws,
All moral canons eager now to waive,
Save only those that wanton Nature gave,
The Nine are grown a thousand! — and the Earth
Hails every morning yet another birth!

 What hinders then, when every youth may choose
As Fancy bids, a musket or a muse,

And throw his lead among his fellow-men,
From the dark muzzle of a gun or pen;
When blooming school-girls, who absurdly think
That nought but drapery can be spoiled with ink,
Ply ceaseless quills that, true to early use,
Keep the old habit of the pristine goose,
While each, a special Sappho in her teens,
Shines forth a goddess in the magazines;
When waning spinsters, happy to rehearse
Their maiden griefs in doubly grievous verse,
Write doleful ditties, or distressful strains,
To wicked rivals, or unfaithful swains,
Or serenade at night's bewitching noon,
The mythic man whose home is in the moon;
When pattern wives no thrifty arts possess,
Save that of weaving — fustian for the Press;
Write Lyrics, heedless of their scorching buns,
Dress up their Sonnets, but neglect their sons,
Make dainty dough-nuts from Parnassian wheat,
And fancy-stockings for poetic feet;
While husbands, — those who love their coffee hot,
And like no 'fire' that doesn't boil the pot, —
Wish old Apollo, just to plague his life,
Had, for his own, a literary wife!
  What hinders then that I, a sober elf,
Who, like the others, keep a Muse myself,

Should venture here, as kind occasion lends
A fitting time to please these urgent friends,
To waive at once my modest Muse's doubt,
And, jockey-like, to trot the lady out? —
An honest creature, I am bound to say,
Who does her duty in a roughish way;
A laughing jade of not ungentle mould,
Although, in sooth, she's something apt to scold,
And, like some worthy people you have seen,
Who're always talking sharper than they mean,
A genuine Sphinx as ever poet sung,
With much good nature and a shrewish tongue!
Yet, like your neighbor, be it understood,
She never censures but for public good,
And like her, too, would feel herself unsexed
If voted angry when she's only vexed!

Don't let me rouse unreasonable fears,
While I, like Brutus, ask you for your ears;
Bear as you can the transient twinge of pain,
In half an hour you'll have them back again.

We're a vast people — that's beyond a doubt —
And nothing loath to let the secret out!
Vain were his labors who should now begin
To stop our growth, or fence the country in!

Let the bold sceptic who denies our worth,
Just hear it proved on any 'Glorious Fourth,'
When patriot-tongues the thrilling tale rehearse
In grand orations, or resounding verse;
When poor John Bull beholds his navies sink
Before the blast, in swelling floods of ink,
And vents his wrath till all around is blue,
To see his armies yearly flogged anew;
While honest Dutchmen, round the speaker's stand,
Forget, for once, their dearer father-land;
And thrifty Caledonians bless the fate
That gives them freedom at so cheap a rate,
And a clear right to celebrate the day,
And not a baubee for the boon to pay;
And Gallia's children prudently relieve
Their bursting bosoms, with as loud a 'vive'
For 'L'Amérique,' as when their voices swell
With equal glory for 'la bagatelle;'
And ardent sons of Erin's blesséd Isle,
Grow patriotic in the Celtic style,
And, all for friendship, bruise each other's eyes,
As when Saint Patrick claims the sacrifice;
While thronging Yankees, all intent to hear
As if the speaker were an auctioneer,

Swell with the theme, till every mother's son
Feels all his country's magnitude his own!
  You'll hear about that sturdy little flock
Who landed once on Plymouth's barren rock,
Daring the dangers of the angry main,
For civil freedom and for godly gain;
An honest, frugal, hardy, dauntless band,
Who sought a refuge in this Western land,
Where (if their own quaint language I may use
That carried back the first Colonial news,)
'Where all the saints may worship as they wish,
And catch abundance of the finest fish!'
  You'll hear, amazed, the hardships they endured,—
To what untold privations were inured,—
What wondrous feats of stout, herculean toil,
Ere they subdued the savage and the soil,
And drave, at last, the intruding heathen out,
Till Witches, Quakers, all were put to rout!

  Here grant the Muse one moment to explain,
Lest you accuse her of a mocking strain.
I love the Puritan; and from my youth
Was taught to admire his valor and his truth.
The veriest caviller must acknowledge still
His honest purpose, and his manly will.

I own I reverence that peculiar race
Who valued steeples less than Christian grace,
Preferred a hut where frost and freedom reigned,
To sumptuous halls at freedom's cost obtained,
And proudly scorning all that royal knaves,
For bartered conscience sold to cringing slaves,
Gave up their homes for rights respected more
Than all the allurements of their native shore,
In stranger lands their tattered flag unfurled,
And taught this doctrine to a startled world:
'Mitres and thrones are man-created things, —
We own no master, save the King of kings!'

'Tis little marvel that their honored name
Bears, as it must, some maculæ of shame;
'Tis only pity that they e'er forgot
The golden lessons their experience taught;
Thought 'Toleration' due to 'saints' alone,
And 'Rights of Conscience' only meant their own!
Enforcing laws, concocted to their need,
On all nonjurors to the ruling creed,
Till Baptists groaned beneath their iron heel,
And Quakers quaked with unaccustomed zeal!

And when I hear, as oft the listener may
In song and sermon on a festal day,

Their virtues lauded to the wondering skies,
As none were e'er so great, or good, or wise,
I straight bethink me of the Irish wit,
(A people famed for many a ready hit,)
Who, sitting once, and rather ill at ease,
To hear, in prose, such huge hyperboles,
Gave for a toast, to chide the fulsome tone,
'Old Plymouth Rock, — the Yankee Blarney-stone!'

But to resume, — as other preachers say,
Led by their twentieth episode astray,
And thus recall their pristine theme anew,
Lost in the mazes of the shifting view, —
But to resume: these hardy pioneers
Grow, in the flight of scarce a hundred years,
Till where a few weak colonies were seen,
Thrive in their strength 'the glorious Old Thirteen;'
And these, anon, released from British rule,
Swarm like the pupils of a parish school;
And still they flourish at a wondrous rate,
Towns follow towns, and state succeeds to state,
Until, at last, among its crimson bars,
Our country's banner, crowded full of stars,
O'er Freedom's sons in happy triumph waves,
Some twenty millions, — not to count the slaves!

We're fond of Missions, and rejoice to lend
Our ready aid the Gospel light to send
To chase the gloom that clouds the Pagan's soul,
And haply make his broken spirit whole;
To take the wanderer led by sin astray,
And win his footsteps to the better way.
No cavilling voice at schemes like this I raise, —
All this is well, and to the nation's praise.
Still let the work with growing force proceed,
That kindly answers to the Heathen's need.
But O, that some brave proselyte would come
And preach good moral's to the folks at home!
O, that the next Australian whom they get
Safe in the meshes of the Gospel net,
Straight to our country may be kindly brought,
With all the Christian doctrine he has got,
That he may teach it, uncorrupt, and clear
Of all perversion, to our Heathen here!
Accursed War, and deadly lust of Gold,
These and their horrors let his eyes behold,
Now, — in the moral summer of the days, —
Here, — in the focus of the Gospel blaze, —
How would he beg the doctors to explain,
And solve the puzzle ere it turned his brain!
And when their best excuses he had heard,
How would his breast with honest zeal be stirred

To teach our graduates in the Christian school
The simple lessons of the Golden Rule!
And how, the while he spoke with pleasure true,
As one unfolding something good and new,
How would the wings of his amazement soar
To find their ears had heard it all before!

O, murderous War! how long shall History choose
Thee for the favorite topic of her muse?
As if the real business of mankind,
The noblest purpose of the immortal mind,
Were shown in him who has the greatest skill
In that old mystery — the art to kill!
And he adorned with most heroic grace,
Who deals the largest slaughter to the race!

A neighboring people rich in landed spoils,
But weak with ignorance and domestic broils,
A haughty nation, full of pride for what
Their fathers were, although themselves are not;
A people fond of pageants and parade,
Replete at once with gas and gasconade,
With all the vapor of the Spanish sire,
Without a flicker of Castilian fire, —
A race like this, — O tell it not in Gath!
Excites our avarice and provokes our wrath,

And so we loose the fiendish dogs of war,
And ply our stripes to gain another star!

Tell not, ye Rabbies of the whiggish creed,
Who trim your doctrines to your party's need,
And let your lips with fluent phrases move
To censure measures which your acts approve,—
Tell not, except to credulous marines,
How you abhor our recent warlike scenes,
And don't again repeat that precious joke
Which gives the odium *all* to Col. Polk,
For he may find who probes the matter well,
At least a dozen Colonels in the shell!
Pray just review the leaders of the bands,
And, as you pass them, let them raise their hands;
Count well the blades that glitter in the sun,
And mark their gallant bearers, one by one,—
For every whig whose sword your eye may catch,
You'll scarcely find a 'loco-foco' match!
We're all alike,—no thinking man defines
The people's temper by their party lines.
With bright exceptions, few and far between,
Like spots of verdure in a winter scene,
From Rio Grandé to Penobscot's flood,
The whole vast nation loves the smell of blood!

But wars cost money; and though fond of wars,
We worship Mammon quite as much as Mars,
And so consent the battle to forego,
And wait till Interest justifies the blow.
Meantime, though Mars upon the shelf is laid,
We yet can summon Draco to our aid.
The cockpit's vulgar; and the pleasant game
Of baiting bears is reckoned much the same;
'The manly Ring' is held improper, too;
The Duel's wicked, and will never do;
'Tis plain to see as any comet's tail,
That war's immoral on so small a scale!
But Draco's grave, decorous and discreet,
And gives diversions in a mode so neat,
'The most fastidious,' — in the showman phrase, —
Can't be offended with his bloody ways.
For, like the doctors, though he cut and bleed,
He shows a broad diploma for the deed!
As boys expend their zoölogic rage
On annual tigers in a travelling cage,
So, by the strictest pathologic rule,
A monthly hanging keeps the nation cool!

The public right to guard the common weal
From thief and ruffian, nought but maniac zeal

Will e'er deny, while every worthy cause
Rests in the proper sanction of the laws.
But when will men the Christian lesson learn,
That 'tis not theirs to throttle or to burn
Their brother sinner to his mortal hurt,
Only because they deem it his desert?
If no stern need, with loud imperious call,
Demand the forfeit, be it great or small,
Let not your heart usurp the sacred throne
Of Him who said that vengeance was his own!
In meek submission drop the uplifted rod,
And leave the sinner to the sinner's God!

In vain we boast the freedom Nature gave,
Alas, the Ethiop's not the only slave!
When from their chains shall Saxon minds be freed,
The slaves to lust, to party, and to creed?

Slaves to their Clique, who favor or oppose
As crafty leaders pull the party-nose;
While the 'dear country,' as the reader learns,[1]
Is saved or ruined in quadrennial turns!

Slaves to the Mode, who pinch the aching waist
And mend God's image to the Gallic taste;
Who sell their comfort for a narrow boot,
Nor heed the 'corn-laws' of the suffering foot!

Slaves to the ruling Sentiment, whose choice
Is but the echo of the public voice,
While their own thoughts the wretches fear to speak,[2]
Not Sundays only, but throughout the week!

Slaves to Antiquity, who put their trust
In mouldy dogmas, mummies, moth, and rust;
Who buy old nothings at the highest cost,
And deem no art worth having till it's lost!

Slaves to their Sect, who deem all heavenly light
Through one small taper cheers the moral night,—
Which, should it fail to throw its radiant spark,
Would leave the hapless nations in the dark!

Slaves to Consistency and prudent fears,
As if mistakes grew sacred with their years!
Fearful of change, and much ashamed to show
They're wiser now than twenty years ago,
Because, forsooth, 'twould make the matter plain
They once were wrong, and may be so again!

Slaves to Ambition and the lust of fame
Who sell their substance for a shadowy name,
And barter happy years for one brief hour
Of courtly dalliance with the harlot, Power!

Bond slaves to Avarice, who perversely soil
Their willing hands with hard, unceasing toil,

For no reward except the menial strife,
As knaves turn tread-mills in a convict life!

But least the Muse should give her hearers pain
By overstraining her heroic strain,—
A metre strong and well-contrived, in sooth,
To bear full measures of satiric truth,
But rather grave, and something apt to tire
Those ears perverse that love an easy lyre,—
She'll drop the proud heroic for a while
For a new topic and a nimbler style,
And, just for change, endeavor to unfold
The shining treasures of the Land of Gold!

EL DORADO.

1.

Hurrah for the land where the moor and the mountain
Are sparkling with treasures no language hath told,
Where the wave of the river and spray of the fountain,
Are bright with the glitter of genuine gold!
Who cares for the pleasures and duties of home,
And all the refinements that grow in its bowers?
To the happy Dorado away we will roam,
'Twill be time to 'refine' when the metal is ours!

2.

Hurrah for the country where Mercury and Mammon
Are the rulers enthroned in the Capitol-seat;
Where Order is chaos, and Justice is gammon,
And yet there's no Bacon to read or to eat!
Let Famine stalk gaunt and ungainly around,
So thin that his features you scarce can behold,—
Who'd live upon bread at an ounce for a pound?
Or exchange for potatoes his carats of gold?

3.

Hurrah for the country where Ceres and Hymen
Are driven abashed from the bountiful soil,
And Music's unheard, save the musical chiming
Of pickaxe and pan in the clatter of toil.
Who cares for your dull academical lore?
Or would seek for a single philosopher's stone,
When out of the heaps of auriferous ore
He can fill up his pockets with 'rocks' of his own?

4.

Hurrah for the country where Plutus is chief,
And where for a wonder especially odd,
His worshippers freely avow their belief,
And are never ashamed to acknowledge their god!

Where the currency's ruled by a natural law,
   And Biddles and Barings are voted no thanks,
Where, in spite of the heavy, perpetual draw,
   There's always abundance of gold in the Banks!

5.

If a brother seduced by our precious estate,
   And mad with the frenzy that lucre inspires,
Should hit us, some day, on the back of the pate,
   With a heartier thump than affection requires,
And our bodies be hid in the glittering dust,—
   What matters the incident? why should we care?
To die very rich is the national lust,
   To be 'buried in gold' is the popular prayer!

6.

Then away with all doubting and fanciful ills,
   Away with impressions that duty would print,
The Pactolian drops that affection distils
   Can never be coined into drops of the mint!
So hurrah for the land where the moor and the mountain
   Are sparkling with treasures no tongue can unfold,
Where the wave of the river and spray of the fountain,
   Are bright with the glitter of genuine gold!

Let others, dazzled by the shining ore,
Delve in the dirt to gather golden store.
Let others, patient of the menial toil
And daily suffering, seek the precious spoil;
While most shall struggle through the weary years,
With naught of Midas save his ample ears!
No hero I, in such a case to brave
Hunger and pain, the robber and the grave.
I'll work, instead, exempt from hate and harm,
The fruitful 'placers' of my mountain-farm,
Where the bright ploughshare opens richest veins,
From whence shall issue countless golden grains,
Which, in the fulness of the year, shall come
In bounteous sheaves, to bless my harvest-home!

But, haply, good may come of mining yet;
'Twill help to pay the nation's foreign debt;
'Twill further liberal arts; plate rings and pins,
Gild books and coaches, mirrors, signs and sins;
'Twill cheapen pens and pencils, and perchance
May give us honest dealing for Finance.
(That magic art, unknown to darker times
When fraud and falsehood were reputed crimes,
Whose curious laws with nice precision teach
How whole estates are made from parts of speech;

How lying rags for honest coin shall pass,
And foreign gold be paid in native brass!)
'Twill save, perhaps, each deep-indebted State
From all temptation to 'repudiate,'
Till Time restore our precious credit lost,
And hush the wail of Peter Plymley's ghost![3]

But lest, O Muse, thy weary friends complain
Thou lovest o'ermuch the harsh satiric strain;
Perversely pleased with hateful themes alone,
And ever singing in a scolding tone,
E'en change the note, and dedicate thy lays
For one brief moment to discerning praise.

While drones and dreaming optimists protest
'The worst is well, and all is for the best;'
And sturdy croakers chant the counter song,
That 'man grows worse, and every thing is wrong;'
Truth, as of old, still loves a golden mean,
And shuns extremes to walk erect between!
The world improves; with slow, unequal pace,
'The Good Time's coming' to our hapless race.
The general tide beneath the refluent surge
Rolls on, resistless, to its destined verge!
Unfriendly hills no longer interpose[4]
As stubborn walls to geographic foes,

Nor envious streams run only to divide
The hearts of brethren ranged on either side.
Promethean Science, with untiring eye
Searching the mysteries of the earth and sky;
And cunning Art, with strong and plastic hand
To work the marvels Science may command;
And broad-winged Commerce, swift to carry o'er
Earth's countless blessings to her farthest shore,—
These, and no German, nor Genevan sage,
These are the great reformers of the age!
  See Art, exultant in her stately car,
On Nature's Titans wage triumphant war!
While e'en the Lightnings by her wondrous skill
Are tamed for heralds of her sovereign will!
Old Ocean's breast a new invader feels,
And heaves in vain to clog her iron wheels·
In vain the Forests marshal all their force,
And Mountains rise to stay her onward course;
From out her path each bold opposer hurled,
She throws her girdle round a captive world!

  I've kept my promise. Of a prosy song
Men want but little, nor that little long
Yet even dulness may afford relief
On some occasions, if it's only brief;

As transient cloudlets soothe the aching sight,
Blind with the dazzle of untempered light!
'Tis something that my Pegasus, though slow,
Don't stand curvetting when he's bid to go;
And clear at least of one egregious fault,
Knows like a Major when and where to halt!
If in his flight he ventured not to soar
Where Helios' son, too rashly, went before,
(A pregnant hint for feeble bards who dare
The awful heights beyond their native air,)
'Twas no dull spirit held the nag in check,
But only mercy for his rider's neck,—
Whom, were he lost among the fogs that lie
Between the empyrean and the nether sky,
And headlong hurled to some Bœotian deep,
No pitying nymphs had gathered round to weep![5]

NOTES.

NOTE 1. Page 143.

While the dear country, as the reader learns,
Is saved or ruined in quadrennial turns.

It is certainly very notable that the difference between the country's 'ruin' and 'salvation' by the vicissitudes of politics, is so little obvious to the mere observer of national affairs, that he would scarcely know when to weep or rejoice, but for the timely information afforded by his party newspaper!

NOTE 2. Page 144.

While their own thoughts the wretches fear to speak,
Not Sundays only, but throughout the week.

An allusion to the Scriptural injunction, 'not to speak one's own words' on the Sabbath day.

NOTE 3. Page 149.

And hush the wail of Peter Plymley's ghost.

Rev. Sydney Smith, the English author and wit, lately deceased, who having speculated in Pennsylvania Bonds to the damage of his estate, berated 'the rascally repudiators' with much spirit, and lamented his losses in many excellent jests.

NOTE 4. Page 149.

Unfriendly hills no longer interpose
As stubborn walls to geographic foes,
Nor envious streams run only to divide
The hearts of brethren ranged on either side.

Lands intersected by a narrow frith
Abhor each other. Mountains interposed
Make enemies of nations, who had else
Like kindred drops been mingled into one.'

NOTE 5. Page 151.

No pitying nymphs had gathered round to weep.

It is a part of the fable of Phæthon, the son of Helios, of whom mention is made a few lines above, that, when he had fallen from the sky and was drowned in the river Eridanus, his sisters, the Heliades, assembling on the shore, lamented his fate in tears, which were changed to amber as they fell.

CARMEN LÆTUM:

Recited, after dinner, before the Alumni of Middlebury College, at their Semi-centennial Celebration, August 22d, 1850.

A RIGHT loving welcome, my true-hearted Brothers,
Who have come out to visit the kindest of mothers;
You may think as you will, but there isn't a doubt
Alma Mater rejoices, and knows you are out!
Rejoices to see you in gratitude here,
Returning to honor her fiftieth year.
And while the good lady is so overcome
With maternal emotion, she's stricken quite dumb,
(A thing, I must own, that's enough to perplex
A shallow observer, who thinks that the sex,
Whatever may be their internal revealings,
Can never be pained with unspeakable feelings,)
Indulge me, dear Brothers, nor think me ill-bred,
If I venture a moment to speak in her stead.

I, who, though the humblest and homeliest one,
Feel the natural pride of a dutiful son,
And esteem it to-day the profoundest of joys,
That, not less than yourselves, I am one of the boys!

First as to her health, which, I'm sorry to say,
Has been better, no doubt, than she finds it to-day:
Yet when you reflect she's been somewhat neglected,
She's really as well as could well be expected;
And, spite of ill-treatment and premature fears,
Is a hearty old lady, for one of her years.
Indeed, I must tell you a bit of a tale,
To show you she's feeling remarkably hale;
How she turned up her nose, but a short time ago,
At a rather good-looking, importunate beau,
And how she refused with a princess-like carriage,
'A very respectable offer of marriage!'[1]

You see, my dear Brothers, a neighboring College,
Who values himself on the depth of his knowledge,

---

[1] Allusion is had in this, and subsequent lines, to an unsuccessful attempt to unite Middlebury College with the University of Vermont. The affair is here treated with the license of a dinner-poem, and with the partiality permitted to the occasion.

With a prayer for her love, and eye to her land,
Walked up to the lady and offered his hand.
For a minute or so, she was all in a flutter,
And had not a word she could audibly utter;
For she felt in her bosom, beyond all concealing,
A kind of a — sort of a — widow-like feeling!
But recovering soon from the delicate shock,
She held up her head like an old-fashioned clock,
And with proper composure, went on and defined
In suitable phrases, the state of her mind;
Said she wouldn't mind changing her single condition,
Could she fairly expect to improve her position;
And thus, by some words of equivocal scope,
Gave her lover decided 'permission to hope.'
It were idle to talk of the billing and cooing
The amorous gentleman used in his wooing;
Or how she replied to his pressing advances,
His *os*cular touches and ocular glances; —
'Tis enough that his courtship, by all that is known,
Was quite the old story, and much like your own!

Thus the matter went on, till the lady found out,
One very fine day, what the rogue was about, —
That all that he wanted was merely the power
By marital license to pocket her dower,

And then to discard her in sorrow and shame,
Bereaved of her home and her name and her fame.
In deep indignation she turned on her heel,
With such withering scorn as a lady might feel
For a knave, who, in stealing her miniature case,
Should take the gold setting, and leave her the face!
But soon growing calm as the breast of the deep,
When the breezes are hushed that the waters may sleep,
She sat in her chair, like a dignified elf,
And thus, while I listened, she talked to herself: —
'Nay, 'twas idle to think of so foolish a plan
As a match with this pert University-man,
For I haven't a chick but would redden with shame,
At the very idea of my losing my name;
And would feel that no sorrow so heavy could come
To his mother, as losing her excellent home.
'Tis true I am weak, but my children are strong,
And won't see me suffer privation or wrong;
So, away with the dream of connubial joys,
I'll stick to the homestead, and look to the boys!'

How joyous, my friends, is the cordial greeting
Which gladdens the heart at a family meeting;
When brothers assemble at Friendship's old shrine,
To look at the present, and talk of 'Lang Syne!'

Ah! well I remember the halcyon years,
Too earnest for laughter, too pleasant for tears,
When life was a boon in yon classical court,
Though lessons were long, and though commons were
short!
Ah! well I remember those excellent men,
Professors and tutors, who reigned o'er us then;
Who guided our feet over Science's bogs,
And led us quite safe through Philosophy's fogs.
Ah! well I remember the President's* face,
As he sat at the lecture with dignified grace,
And neatly unfolded the mystical themes
Of various deep metaphysical schemes, —
How he brightened the path of his studious flock,
As he gave them a key to that wonderful *Locke;*
How he taught us to feel it was fatal indeed,
With too much reliance to lean upon *Reid;*
That *Stewart* was sounder, but wrong at the last,
From following his master a little too fast, —
Then closed the discourse in a scholarly tone,
With a clear and intelligent creed of his own.
That the man had his faults it were safe to infer, —
Though I really don't recollect what they were, —

* Joshua Bates, D. D.

I barely remember this one little truth,
When his case was discussed by the critical youth,
The Seniors and Freshmen were sure to divide,
And the former were all on the President's side!

And well I remember another, whose praise
Were a suitable theme for more elegant lays;
But even in numbers ungainly and rough,
I must mention the name of our glorious HOUGH!
Who does not remember? for who can forget,
Till Memory's star shall forever have set,
How he sat in his place, unaffected and bold,
And taught us more truths than the lesson had told?
Gave a lift to 'Old NOL,' for the love of the right,
And a slap at the Stuarts, with cordial spite;
And quite in the teeth of conventional rules,
Hurled his adjectives down upon tyrants and fools?
But, chief, he excelled in his proper vocation
Of giving the classics a classic translation;
In Latin and Greek he was almost oracular,
And, what's more to his praise, understood the vernacular
Oh! 'twas pleasant to hear him make English of Greek,
Till you felt that no tongue was inherently weak;
While Horace in Latin seemed quite understated,
And rejoiced like old Enoch in being translated!

And others there were, but the hour would fail,
To bring them all up in historic detail;
And yet I would give, ere the moment has fled,
A sigh for the absent, a tear for the dead.
There's not one of them all, where'er he may rove,
In the shadows of earth, or the glories above,
In the home of his birth, or in lands far away,
But comes back to be kindly remembered to-day!

One little word more, and my duty is done; —
A health to our Mother, from each mother's son!
Unfading in beauty, increasing in strength,
May she flourish in health through the century's length!
And next when her children come round her to boast,
May *Esto perpetua* then be the toast!

THE DEVIL OF NAMES.

A LEGEND.

At an old-fashioned inn with a pendulous sign,
Once graced with the head of the king of the kine,
But innocent now of the slightest 'design,'
Save calling low people to spurious wine —
While the villagers, drinking and playing 'all fours,'
And cracking small jokes, with vociferous roars,
Were talking of horses, and hunting, and — scores
Of similar topics a bar-room adores,
But which rigid morality greatly deplores,
Till as they grew high in their bacchanal revels,
They fell to discoursing of witches and devils —
　　　　A neat single rap,
　　　　Just the ghost of a tap,
That would scarcely have wakened a flea from his nap,

Not at all in its sound like your 'Rochester Knocking,'
(Where asses in herds are diurnally flocking,)
But twice as mysterious, and vastly more shocking,
Was heard at the door by the people within,
Who stopped in a moment their clamorous din,
And ceased in a trice from their jokes and their gin;
When who should appear
But an odd-looking stranger somewhat 'in the sere,'
(He seemed at the least in his sixtieth year,)
And he limped in a manner exceedingly queer,
Wore breeches uncommonly wide in the rear,
And his nose was turned up with a comical sneer,
And he had in his eye a most villanous leer,
Quite enough to make any one tremble with fear!
Whence he came,
And what was his name,
And what his purpose in venturing out,
And whether his lameness was 'gammon' or gout,
Or merely fatigue from strolling about,
Were questions involved in a great deal of doubt —
When taking a chair,
With a sociable air,
Like that which your 'Uncle' 's accustomed to wear,
Or a broker determined to sell you a share
In his splendid 'New England Gold-mining' affair,
He opened his mouth and went on to declare

That he was a *devil* — 'The devil you are!'
Cried one of the guests assembled there,
With a sudden start, and a frightened stare!
'Nay, don't be alarmed,' the stranger exclaims,
'At the name of the devil — *I'm the Devil of Names!*
You'll wonder why
Such a devil as I,
Who ought, you would say, to be devilish shy,
Should venture in here with never a doubt,
And let the best of his secrets out;
But mind you, my boys,
It's one of the joys
Of the cunningest woman and craftiest man,
To run as quickly as ever they can,
And put a confidant under ban
Not to publish their favorite plan!
And even the de'il
Will sometimes feel
A little of that remarkable zeal,
And (when it's safe) delights to tell
The very deepest *arcana* of — well —
Besides, my favor this company wins,
For I value next to capital sins,
Those out-and-outers who revel in inns!
So, not to delay,
I'm going to say

In the very fullest and frankest way,
All about my honors and claims,
Projects and plans, and objects and aims,
And *why* I'm called "The Devil of Names!"
I cheat by false graces,
And duplicate faces,
And treacherous praises,
And by hiding bad things under plausible phrases!
I'll give you a sample,
By way of example —
Here's a bottle before me, will suit to a T
For a nice illustration — this liquor, d'ye see,
Is the water of death, though topers agree
To think it, and drink it as pure "*eau de vie;*"
I know what it is — that's sufficient for me!
For the blackest of sins, and crimes, and shames,
I find soft words and innocent names.
The Hells devoted to Satan's games
I christen "Saloons" and "Halls," and then,
By another contrivance of mine again,
They're only haunted by "sporting men" —
A phrase which many a gamester begs,
In spite of the saw that "eggs is eggs,"
To whiten his nigritudinous legs!

'To debauchees I graciously grant
The favor to be "a little gallant,"
And soften vicious vagrancy down,
By civilly speaking of "men about town;"
    There's cheating and lying
    In selling and buying,
And all sorts of frauds and dishonest exactions,
I've brought to the smallest of moral infractions,
Merely by naming them "business transactions!"
There's swindling, now, is vastly more fine
As "Banking"— a lucky invention of mine,
Worth ten in the *old* diabolical line!

'In lesser matters it's all the same,
I gain the thing by yielding the name;
It's really quite the broadest of jokes —
But, on my honor, there's plenty of folks
So uncommonly fond of verbal cloaks,
They can't enjoy the dinners they eat,
Court the "muse of the twinkling feet,"
Laugh or sing, or do any thing meet
For Christian people, without a cheat
To make their happiness quite complete!
    The Boston saints
    Are fond of these feints;

A theatre rouses the loudest complaints,
Till it's thoroughly purged from pestilent taints,
By the charm of a name and a pious *Te Deum* —
Yet they patronize actors, and handsomely fee 'em!
Keep (shade of "the Howards!" (a gay "Athenæum,"
And have, above all, a harmless "Museum,"
Where folks who love plays may religiously see 'em!

'But leaving a trifle which costs me more trouble
By far than the worth of so flimsy a bubble,
I come to a matter which really claims
The studious care of the Devil of Names.
There's "Charity" now —'

But the lecture was done,
Like old Goody Morey's, when scarcely begun;
The devil's discourse by its serious teaching
Had set 'em a-snoring, like regular preaching!
One look of disdain on the sleepers he threw,
As in bitter contempt of the slumbering crew,
And the devil had vanished without more ado —
A trick, I suspect, that he seldom plays you!

TRAVESTIES.

PHAETHON;

OR THE AMATEUR COACHMAN.

Dan Phaëthon, — so the histories run, —
Was a jolly young chap, and a son of the Sun;
Or rather of Phœbus, — but as to his mother,
Genealogists make a deuse of a pother,
Some going for one, and some for another!
For myself, I must say, as a careful explorer,
This roaring young blade was the son of Aurora!

Now old Father Phœbus, ere railways begun
To elevate funds and depreciate fun,
Drove a very fast coach by the name of 'The Sun;'
Running, they say,
Trips every day,
(On Sundays and all, in a heathenish way,)
All lighted up with a famous array

Of lanterns that shone with a brilliant display,
And dashing along like a gentleman's 'shay,'
With never a fare, and nothing to pay!
Now PHAËTHON begged of his doting old father,
To grant him a favor, and this the rather,
Since some one had hinted, the youth to annoy,
That he wasn't by any means PHŒBUS's boy!
Intending, the rascally son of a gun,
To darken the brow of the son of the SUN!
'By the terrible Styx!' said the angry sire,
While his eyes flashed volumes of fury and fire,
'To prove your reviler an infamous liar,
I swear I will grant you whate'er you desire!'
'Then by my head,'
The youngster said,
'I'll mount the coach when the horses are fed! —
For there's nothing I'd choose, as I'm alive,
Like a seat on the box, and a dashing drive!'
'Nay, PHAËTHON, don't, —
I beg you won't, —
Just stop a moment and think upon't!'
'You're quite too young,' continued the sage,
'To tend a coach at your tender age!
Besides, you see,
'Twill really be
Your first appearance on any stage!

Desist, my child,
The cattle are wild,
And when their mettle is thoroughly " riled,"
Depend upon't, the coach'll be " spiled " —
They're not the fellows to draw it mild!
Desist, I say,
You'll rue the day, —
So mind, and don't be foolish, PHA! '
But the youth was proud,
And swore aloud,
'Twas just the thing to astonish the crowd, —
He'd have the horses and wouldn't be cowed!
In vain the boy was cautioned at large,
He called for the chargers, unheeding the charge,
And vowed that any young fellow of force,
Could manage a dozen coursers, of course!
Now PHŒBUS felt exceedingly sorry
He had given his word in such a hurry,
But having sworn by the Styx, no doubt
He was in for it now, and couldn't back out.
So calling PHAËTHON up in a trice,
He gave the youth a bit of advice : —
' " *Parce stimulis, utere loris!* "
(A " stage direction," of which the core is,

Don't use the whip, — they're ticklish things, —
But, whatever you do, hold on to the strings!)
Remember the rule of the Jehu-tribe is,
"*Medio tutissimus ibis*,"
(As the Judge remarked to a rowdy Scotchman,
Who was going to quod between two watchmen!)
So mind your eye, and spare your goad,
Be shy of the stones, and keep in the road!'

Now PHAËTHON, perched in the coachman's place,
Drove off the steeds at a furious pace,
Fast as coursers running a race,
Or bounding along in a steeple-chase!
Of whip and shout there was no lack,
'Crack — whack —
Whack — crack'
Resounded along the horses' back! —
Frightened beneath the stinging lash,
Cutting their flanks in many a gash,
On — on they sped as swift as a flash,
Through thick and thin away they dash,
(Such rapid driving is always rash!)
When all at once, with a dreadful crash,
The whole 'establishment' went to smash!
And PHAËTHON, he,
As all agree,

Off the coach was suddenly hurled,
Into a puddle, and out of the world!

MORAL.

Don't rashly take to dangerous courses, —
Nor set it down in your table of forces,
That any one man equals any four horses!
        Don't swear by the Styx! —
        It's one of OLD NICK'S
        Diabolical tricks
To get people into a regular 'fix,'
And hold 'em there as fast as bricks!

PYRAMUS AND THISBE.

This tragical tale, which, they say, is a true one,
Is old, but the manner is wholly a new one.
One *Ovid*, a writer of some reputation,
Has told it before in a tedious narration ;
In a style, to be sure, of remarkable fulness,
But which nobody reads on account of its dulness.

Young Peter Pyramus — *I* call him *Peter*,
Not for the sake of the rhyme or metre,
But merely to make the name completer —
For Peter lived in the olden times,
And in one of the worst of Pagan climes
That flourish now in classical fame,
        Long before
        Either noble or boor
Had such a thing as a *Christian* name —
Young Peter then was a nice young beau
As any young lady would wish to know ;

In years, I ween,
He was rather green,
That is to say, he was just eighteen, —
A trifle too short, and a shaving too lean,
But 'a nice young man' as ever was seen,
And fit to dance with a May-day queen!

Now PETER loved a beautiful girl
As ever insnared the heart of an earl,
In the magical trap of an auburn curl, —
A little MISS THISBE who lived next door,
(They slept in fact on the very same floor,
With a wall between them, and nothing more, —
Those double dwellings were common of yore,)
And they loved each other, the legends say
In that very beautiful, bountiful way,
That every young maid,
And every young blade,
Are wont to do before they grow staid,
And learn to love by the laws of trade.
But alack-a-day, for the girl and boy,
A little impediment checked their joy,
And gave them, a while, the deepest annoy.
For some good reason which history cloaks,
The match didn't happen to please the old folks!

So THISBE's father and PETER's mother
Began the young couple to worry and bother,
And tried their innocent passion to smother
By keeping the lovers from seeing each other!
But who ever heard
Of a marriage deterred,
Or even deferred,
By any contrivance so very absurd
As scolding the boy, and caging his bird? —
Now PETER, who wasn't discouraged at all
By obstacles such as the timid appall,
Contrived to discover a hole in the wall,
Which wasn't so thick
But removing a brick
Made a passage — though rather provokingly small.
Through this little chink the lover could greet her,
And secrecy made their courting the sweeter,
While PETER kissed THISBE, and THISBE kissed
PETER, —
For kisses, like folks with diminutive souls,
Will manage to creep through the smallest of holes!

'Twas here that the lovers, intent upon love,
Laid a nice little plot
To meet at a spot
Near a mulberry tree in a neighboring grove;

For the plan was all laid,
By the youth and the maid,
(Whose hearts, it would seem, were uncommonly bold ones,)
To run off and get married in spite of the old ones.

In the shadows of evening, as still as a mouse,
The beautiful maiden slipt out of the house,
The mulberry-tree impatient to find,
While PETER, the vigilant matrons to blind,
Strolled leisurely out some minutes behind.

While waiting alone by the trysting tree,
A terrible lion
As e'er you set eye on,
Came roaring along quite horrid to see,
And caused the young maiden in terror to flee,
(A lion's a creature whose regular trade is
Blood — and 'a terrible thing among ladies,')
And losing her veil as she ran from the wood,
The monster bedabbled it over with blood.

Now PETER arriving, and seeing the veil
All covered o'er,
And reeking with gore,

Turned all of a sudden exceedingly pale,
And sat himself down to weep and to wail, —
For, soon as he saw the garment, poor PETER
Made up his mind in very short metre,
That THISBE was dead, and the lion had eat her!
So breathing a prayer,
He determined to share
The fate of his darling, 'the loved and the lost,'
And fell on his dagger, and gave up the ghost!

Now THISBE returning, and viewing her beau,
Lying dead by the veil (which she happened to know)
She guessed, in a moment, the cause of his erring,
And seizing the knife
Which had taken his life,
In less than a jiffy was dead as a herring!

MORAL.

Young gentlemen! — pray recollect, if you please,
Not to make assignations near mulberry-trees.
Should your mistress be missing it shows a weak head
To be stabbing yourself till you know she is dead.

Young ladies! — you shouldn't go strolling about
When your anxious mammas don't know you are out,
And remember that accidents often befall
From kissing young fellows through holes in the wall!

POLYPHEMUS AND ULYSSES.

A VERY remarkable history this is
Of one POLYPHEMUS and Mr. ULYSSES ;
The latter a hero accomplished and bold,
The former a knave and a fright to behold, —
A horrid big giant who lived in a den,
And dined, every day, on a couple of men,
Ate a woman for breakfast, and (dreadful to see !)
Had a nice little baby served up with his tea !
Indeed, if there's truth in the sprightly narration
Of HOMER, a poet of some reputation,
Or VIRGIL, a writer but little inferior,
And in some things, perhaps, the other's superior, —
POLYPHEMUS was truly a terrible creature
In manners and morals, in form and in feature ;
For law and religion he cared not a copper,
And, in short, led a life that was very improper ! —

What made him a very remarkable guy,
Like the late Mr. Thompson, he'd only one eye;
But that was a whopper — a terrible one —
'As large (Virgil says) as the disk of the sun!' —
A brilliant, but rather extravagant figure,
Which means, I suppose, that his eye was much bigger
Than yours — or even the orb of your sly
Old bachelor-friend who's 'a wife in his eye.'

Ulysses, the hero I mentioned before,
Was shipwrecked, one day, on the pestilent shore,
Where the Cyclops resided, along with their chief,
Polyphemus, the terrible man-eating thief,
Whose manners they copied, and laws they obeyed,
While driving their horrible cannibal trade.

With many expressions of civil regret
That Ulysses had got so unpleasantly wet,
With many expressions of pleasure profound
That all had escaped being thoroughly drowned,
The rascal declared he was 'fond of the brave,'
And invited the strangers all home to his cave.

Here the cannibal king, with as little remorse
As an omnibus feels for the death of a horse,

Seized, crushed and devoured a brace of the Greeks,
As a Welshman would swallow a couple of leeks,
Or a Frenchman, supplied with his usual prog,
Would punish the hams of a favorite frog!
Dashed and smashed against the stones,
He broke their bodies and cracked their bones,
Minding no more their moans and groans,
Than the grinder heeds his organ's tones!
With purple gore the pavement swims,
While the giant crushes their crackling limbs,
And poor ULYSSES trembles with fright
At the horrid sound, and the horrid sight,
Trembles lest the monster grim
Should make his 'nuts and raisins' of him!
And, really, since
The man was a Prince,
It's not very odd that his Highness should wince,
(Especially after such very strong hints,)
At the cannibal's manner, as rather more free
Than his Highness, at court, was accustomed to see!

But the crafty Greek, to the tyrant's hurt,
(Though he didn't deserve so fine a dessert,)
Took a dozen of wine from his leather trunk,
And plied the giant until he was drunk!—

Drunker than any one you or *I* know,
Who buys his 'Rhenish' with ready rhino,—
Exceedingly drunk—'*sepultus vino!*'

Gazing a moment upon the sleeper,
ULYSSES cried, 'Let's spoil his peeper!—
'Twill put him, my boys, in a pretty trim,
If we can manage to douse his glim!'
So taking a spar that was lying in sight
They poked it into his 'forward light,'
And gouged away with furious spite,
Ramming and jamming with all their might!

In vain the giant began to roar,
And even swore
That he never before
Had met, in his life, such a terrible bore,—
They only plied the auger the more
And mocked his grief with the bantering cry,
'Don't talk of pain—*it's all in your eye!*'
Until, alas! for the wretched CYCLOPS,
He gives a groan, and out his eye pops!
Leaving the knave, one needn't be told,
As blind as a puppy of three days old!

The rest of the tale I can't tell now —
Except that ULYSSES got out of the row,
With the rest of his crew — it's no matter how;
While old POLYPHEMUS, until he was dead, —
Which wasn't till many years after, 'tis said, —
Had a grief in his heart and a hole in his head!

MORAL.

Don't use strong drink, — pray let me advise, —
It's bad for the stomach, and ruins the eyes;
Don't impose upon sailors with land-lubber tricks,
Or you'll catch it some day, like a thousand of bricks!

ORPHEUS AND EURYDICE.

Sir Orpheus, whom the poets have sung
In every metre and every tongue,
Was, you may remember, a famous musician —
At least for a youth in his pagan condition —
For historians tell he played on his shell
From morning till night so remarkably well
That his music created a regular spell
On trees and stones in forest and dell!
What sort of an instrument his could be
Is really more than is known to me —
For none of the books have told, d'ye see!
It's very certain those heathen 'swells'
Knew nothing at all of oyster-shells,
And it's clear Sir Orpheus never could own a
Shell like those they make in Cremona;
But whatever it was, to 'move the stones'
It must have shelled out some powerful tones,

And entitled the player to rank in my rhyme
As the very *Vieuxtemps* of the very old time!

But, alas for the joys of this mutable life!
Sir Orpheus lost his beautiful wife —
Eurydice — who vanished one day
From Earth, in a very unpleasant way!
It chanced, as near as I can determine,
Through one of those vertebrated vermin
That lie in the grass so prettily curled,
Waiting to 'snake' you out of the world!
And the poets tell she went to — well —
A place where Greeks and Romans dwell
After they burst their mortal shell;
A region that in the deepest shade is,
And known by the classical name of *Hades* —
A different place from the terrible furnace
Of *Tartarus*, down below *Avernus*.

Now, having a heart uncommonly stout,
Sir Orpheus didn't go whining about,
Nor marry another, as *you* would, no doubt,
But made up his mind to fiddle her out!
But near the gate he had to wait,
For there in state old Cerberus sate —

A three-headed dog, as cruel as Fate,
Guarding the entrance early and late;
A beast so sagacious, and very voracious,
So uncommonly sharp and extremely rapacious,
That it really may be doubted whether
He'd have his match, should a common tether
Unite three aldermen's heads together!

But Orpheus, not in the least afraid,
Tuned up his shell, and quickly essayed
What could be done with a serenade.
In short, so charming an air he played,
He quite succeeded in overreaching
The cunning cur, by musical teaching,
And put him to sleep as fast as preaching!

And now our musical champion, Orpheus,
Having given the janitor over to Morpheus,
Went groping around among the ladies
Who throng the dismal halls of Hades,
Calling aloud
To the shady crowd,
In a voice as shrill as a martial fife,
'*O, tell me where in hell is my wife!*'

(A natural question, 'tis very plain,
Although it may sound a little profane.)
'Eurydice, *Eu-ryd-i-ce!*'
He cried as loud as loud could be —
(A singular sound, and funny withal,
In a place where nobody *rides* at all!)
'Eurydice — Eurydice!
O, come, my dear, along with me!'
And then he played so remarkably fine,
That it really might be called divine —
For who can show,
On earth or below,
Such wonderful feats in the musical line?

E'en *Tantalus* ceased from trying to sip
The cup that flies from his arid lip;
Ixion, too, the magic could feel,
And, for a moment, blocked his wheel;
Poor *Sisyphus*, doomed to tumble and toss
The notable 'stone that gathers no moss,'
Let go his burden, and turned to hear
The charming sounds that ravished his ear;
And even the *Furies* — those terrible shrews
Whom no one before could ever amuse —

Those strong-bodied ladies with strong-minded views,
Whom even the devil would doubtless refuse,
Were his majesty only permitted to choose —
Each felt for a moment her nature desert her,
And wept, like a girl o'er the 'Sorrows of Werter!'

And still Sir Orpheus chanted his song,
Sweet and clear and strong and long,
'Eurydice! — Eurydice!'
He cried as loud as loud could be;
And Echo taking up the word,
Kept it up till the lady heard,
And came with joy to meet her lord.
And he led her along the infernal route,
Until he had got her almost out,
When, suddenly turning his head about,
(To take a peep at his wife, no doubt,)
He gave a groan,
For the lady was gone,
And had left him standing there all alone!
For by an oath the gods had bound
Sir Orpheus not to look around
Till he was clear of the sacred ground,
If he'd have Eurydice safe and sound,

For the moment he did an act so rash
His wife would vanish as quick as a flash!

MORAL.

Young women! beware, for goodness' sake,
Of every sort of 'sarpent snake;'
Remember the rogue is apt to deceive,
And played the deuse with Grandmother Eve!
Young men! it's a critical thing to go
Exactly right with a lady in tow;
But when you are in the proper track
Just go ahead, and never look back!

THE END

www.ingramcontent.com/pod-product-compliance
Lightning Source LLC
La Vergne TN
LVHW011224110826
845150LV00006B/1534

* 9 7 8 1 4 2 5 5 1 6 1 9 2 *